Pay-for-Performance Teacher Compensation

An Inside View of Denver's ProComp Plan

Rick —

I can't imagine better than a good tale about the impact you will be has had on Denver.

Get well soon,

Phil Gonring

Cheers Rick — Hope you enjoy the read — get well soon,

Paul

Pay-for-Performance Teacher Compensation

An Inside View of Denver's ProComp Plan

PHIL GONRING, PAUL TESKE, AND BRAD JUPP

HARVARD EDUCATION PRESS

CAMBRIDGE, MASSACHUSETTS

Library of Congress Control Number 2007928174

Paperback ISBN 978-1-891792-43-4
Library Edition ISBN 978-1-891792-44-1

Published by Harvard Education Press,
an imprint of the Harvard Education Publishing Group

Harvard Education Press
8 Story Street
Cambridge, MA 02138

Cover Design: Perry D. Lubin

The typefaces used in this book are ITC Slimbach for text and Castle for display.

Contents

Acknowledgments

We first would like to express our gratitude to the people who provided us with ideas and background information for our book, many of whom played a critical role in making ProComp a reality in Denver Public Schools. In alphabetical order, they include Greg Ahrnsbrak, Beverly Ausfahl, Bruce Benson, Elaine Berman, John Britz, Jeff Buck, Pam Buckley, Sheila Bugdanowitz, Veronica Davey, Bruce Dickinson, Beth Douma, Ed Freeman, Greg Kolomitz, Don Kortz, Chrisanne LaHue, Andre Pettigrew, Irv Moskowitz, Lydia Peña, Henry Roman, Shirley Scott, Steve Shogan, Bill Slotnik, Paul Talmey, Jerry Wartgow, Steve Welchert, Connie White, Ed Wiley, Becky Wissink, and Les Woodward. We offer a special tip of our caps to Bruce Dickinson, who graciously took numerous phone calls to provide background information so that the authors could meet their deadline.

As we will describe later in the book, there is a debate in the field of entrepreneurial policy development about whether it takes a few or many entrepreneurs to create the circumstances for lasting change. Whether the actions of the many who worked on ProComp were entrepreneurial is not our focus here. The point we want to make is that without the actions and vital energy of many teachers, bureaucrats, researchers, consultants, board members, and community and union leaders, we would never have been given the opportunity by Harvard Education Press to write a book. Hopefully, the work demonstrates our high regard for the many teachers and other actors who willed ProComp into being.

Being both authors and subjects of the narrative, Gonring and Jupp sometimes felt a bit awkward in writing the book. However, the power of a three-person collaborative assuages some of that awkwardness. When one author needed to become the subject, another either "handled" the subject or scrutinized the writing to make sure it was fair and accurate.

Gonring certainly enjoyed writing about his friend Brad Jupp. Remarkably, their friendship remains intact.

We want to thank Caroline Chauncey of Harvard Education Press for seeing the potential in our book. She also provided expert guidance in revising our initial drafts and suggesting which of our many sports and transportation metaphors worked better than others. We also greatly appreciate Erin Holman's sensitive copy editing, which sharpened our presentation of ideas, and Dody Riggs's excellent book editing and production management. Phil Nash, vice president of communications of Rose Community Foundation, also generously gave many hours to read and help edit earlier drafts. Finally, we would like to thank Sheila Bugdanowitz, president and CEO of Rose Community Foundation, for giving Gonring the time and space to write the book and for her support of Teske's and Jupp's efforts.

As for the individual coauthors, Gonring would like to thank his children, Dakota and Zoë, for putting up with him while he wrote on weekends and late into many weekday nights. "Don't ever do this again," Dakota advised his father on more than one occasion. He would also like to thank the current and past trustees and education committee members of Rose Community Foundation for having the wisdom and guts to take on and stick with a risky project that many times appeared headed for the scrapheap of education reform. He also cannot say enough about the support he received from Rose Community Foundation's founding and current CEOs, Don Kortz and Sheila Bugdanowitz, who together have created a very special place to work in the field of philanthropy. Finally, he would like to salute his tenth-grade English teacher, Katherine Starkey, who deserves most of the credit for teaching him how to write. Like many of her colleagues at Green Mountain High School and several talented and dedicated educators who taught Gonring's children over the years in Denver Public Schools, she deserved to make a boatload of money.

Teske would like to thank his family--Kim, Julia, and Reid--for understanding his absences on several weekend days to work on the manuscript. He would also like to thank Kathleen Beatty, the dean of the Graduate School of Public Affairs, for her support on this project from start to finish. Like Gonring, Teske was inspired by many wonderful teachers to pursue his own career in research and teaching, but he most recalls Richard Murphy, a tenth-grade social studies teacher at John Jay High School in East Fishkill, New York, who brought American history alive with his intelligence, passion, guitar, and, later, by practicing what he preached as a county legislator.

Jupp would like to thank the many educators, leaders, and unionists who helped clear the path that led to the creation of ProComp and its related reforms. The list is too numerous to name them all and many get their due in the book itself, but he would like to single out two of them. The first is Mel Mickelsen, who helped invent collective bargaining for teachers in Colorado and taught Jupp that a union could negotiate anything it wanted into a labor agreement if it just seized the power. The second is Andrea Giunta, DCTA president through 2001. She deserves credit for her courage, not only because she opened the door to the Pay for Performance Pilot, but because she, along with Bruce Dickinson, cleared the path in Denver for the union to talk about the quality of teaching at the negotiating table. In the end, however, the action of the teachers and voters in Denver was a collective leap of faith. Without the hundreds of individuals who added their hope and credibility to the effort, the leap would have fallen short.

Jupp would also like to thank Gonring and Teske, friends who did good work on this book. Somehow Jupp wonders if authorship is defined as talking on the cell phone to someone who is really doing the writing.

Finally, Jupp would like to thank his wife, Chrisanne LaHue, and stepdaughter, Hilary Johnson, who deserve much more than acknowledgment in a preface. Their love and commitment are boundless. They ate more takeout than any reasonable family should. They took vacations on their own. They helped find common sense when Jupp couldn't find any on his own. Some know that it was LaHue who, in response to the district proposal to implement pay for performance in 1999, said, "Just make the district try it in the schools." Chrisanne has become one of the 1,600 teachers getting paid under the new system; it better work, because it is expected to help put Hilary through college. Theirs is commitment and love that Jupp wishes to equal every day.

Introduction

On February 12, 2004, only 38 days before members of the Denver Classroom Teachers Association (DCTA) were scheduled to vote on the groundbreaking Professional Compensation Plan for teachers (ProComp), polling data suggested that only 19 percent of teachers would vote in favor of the plan. Yet that day in February was not the first on which ProComp appeared to be on its deathbed—nor would it be the last. Nearly two years later, however, the citizens of Denver followed the teachers' own approval of the new system by endorsing ProComp, voting to raise their taxes by $25 million annually to pay for it.

As we write this book, ProComp is in its first year of full implementation. School reformers and school districts across the country are watching to see how ProComp develops and whether it will be a successful venture that helps propel teacher compensation into the twenty-first century. Indeed, interest in ProComp spans the globe, with even the *Beijing Times* reporting on the successful Denver election. And, on November 1, 2006, the U.S. Department of Education announced the first round of grant-making from the new Teacher Incentive Fund, (a program itself created in part due to Denver's success with ProComp), making Denver Public Schools the largest grant recipient, giving the district more than half of first-round funds for ProComp's implementation and extension to principals.

In this book we give a status report on ProComp. But our main goal is to explain how it came into being in Denver, when similar efforts have failed or may not have been attempted for political or pragmatic reasons elsewhere. While the *New York Times* and other national media have

1

chronicled certain stages of ProComp's development or profiled some of the leaders of the Denver effort, none have provided an in-depth, book-length analysis of how ProComp came into being. We hope to provide readers with the inside story of what actually happened in the first eight years of ProComp's development, while at the same time offering some explicit lessons that may spur reform elsewhere. Indeed, reforms modeled after ProComp are already proceeding in Washington, D.C., and Chicago and, at the state level, in Florida.

ProComp is but one exciting new solution to an important question: How should teachers be paid? The question appears simple, but, despite the inclinations of many in the policy arena to address it quickly, its answers are anything but simple. Further, as we will say throughout the book, we do not believe that ProComp is the final solution for teacher compensation reform. It's a step forward, but it will be up to others, in Denver and across the nation, to continue the work.

Like most public employees whose salaries are paid with government tax revenues, for most of the history of public schooling in America, teachers have been paid based on their own inputs—their educational training and especially their years of service. Such has been the lot of Denver teachers. The idea of tying at least some of teachers' pay to outcomes, results, or performance has stood on the extreme fringes of America's more-than-$500-billion public education system. Denver, however, has made considerable progress. Denver teachers have approved a plan that will pay them more if they improve student achievement, acquire and demonstrate new knowledge and skills, choose to work in hard-to-staff schools and positions, and receive satisfactory evaluations. Moreover, the Denver plan is not a straight bonus system, like some that have come before it. Many of the elements allow teachers to build permanent salary increases, and one subcomponent actually requires teachers whose students underperform to lose raises previously earned within the program. Finally, unlike most systems elsewhere, ProComp is not a simple add-on to the single salary schedule; it in fact replaces that artifact altogether.

Let us be clear from the beginning: ProComp is more complex than what is often referred to as "pay for performance" (PFP). To some, PFP has come to suggest that teacher pay should be tied to one outcome only: student achievement. We intend to place ProComp in the PFP tradition, however, using that term more liberally. Someday, as teacher compensation reform unfolds, we will no doubt find another and better term that more accurately expresses changes communities will be making to their salary systems.

As ProComp's complexity and our brief discussion of the language of compensation reform suggest, the major problems with implementing PFP plans in America have been two-fold: technical and political. Regardless of what avid PFP supporters might suggest, it is not easy to figure out the appropriate incentives and tools to pay our most accomplished teachers more than those who are mediocre, or to encourage our nation's best and brightest to enter the profession. Many of us believe we can distinguish easily between great teachers and mediocre or inadequate ones. In fact, however, when one looks at a large number of teachers spread across urban or other sizeable districts, it is not always easy to tell the groups apart, much less to discriminate among finer levels of teaching quality. Until recently, the idea that student learning could be carefully and fairly measured did not have much support, and even now it is somewhat controversial. Other indicators of "good teaching" have been as difficult to quantify as is teachers' connection to increased student achievement. One important reason that previous attempts at PFP plans have failed is that the technical solutions to these measurement problems have not always been good or thoughtful ones.

Despite some real technical issues, most analysts highlight the politics of labor/management relations as the chief obstacle to teacher compensation reform. Unions have preferred across-the-board wage hikes to any form of differentiated pay—especially pay based on student achievement. Some unions also argue that teachers cannot be held responsible for learning outcomes, especially when their students come from disadvantaged backgrounds. Like their counterparts in other employee unions, teacher unions have tended to support standardized pay scales based on educational inputs and years of services, arguing that they provide more stability for their membership and greater rewards for seniority.

So, the generally accepted explanation for why we do not have more diverse compensation systems for teachers in America, one that has much validity, is that teachers unions do not want them. Thus, the idea of Denver teachers embracing ProComp is the most surprising political angle to our story. Yet reformers should note that polling data for Denver voters revealed similar attitudes among the citizenry in advance of the public vote to fund ProComp. Surprisingly, many voters feared that pay for performance would lead to more teaching to the test, a prospect that a large segment of the public finds unacceptable. Moreover, some of the obstacles within the school district offices in Denver were every bit as serious as those within the union halls.

We wrote this book, then, to explain how ProComp developed in Denver and, in particular, how many of these obstacles were overcome. We will tell our story from the vantage point of key actors in the drama, coauthors Phil Gonring and Brad Jupp. Jupp spent 15 years as a union leader and is now an administrator in the Denver Public School system (DPS), helping develop and implement ProComp. Jupp provides the inside story of ProComp from the union perspective, but his new position also provides a wider lens. Gonring and Jupp went through the teacher-education program at the University of Colorado together and student-taught at Denver's George Washington High School, where Gonring taught six years. For the past 10 years, Gonring has been a program officer at Rose Community Foundation, which played an entrepreneurial role in ProComp by investing $4 million, leveraging another $3.5 million in philanthropic funds, and exercising leadership at key stages of ProComp's evolution. Parts of this story could also be told from the perspective of others who played important roles in the development of Denver's salary system—union leaders, teachers, administrators, and school board members—many of whom made tremendous personal sacrifices and took great risks, without which we would have nothing to write about.

In fact, a theme throughout the book is that those working in urban school systems, despite what some may otherwise think, have tremendous genius, a working intelligence that can unfold if it is given the time normally afforded business, industry, and philanthropy. Pro-

Comp's story, we hope, will give other jurisdictions the encouragement that they can take teacher compensation reform to the next step.

To move the story of ProComp beyond the level of an extraordinary case study, and to link to broader notions of how education reform can take place, we also frame the details of the narrative with an entrepreneurial approach to policy development. We highlight the times entrepreneurial actions and strategies were necessary to move ProComp forward. But, in the final chapter of this book, we flesh out this theme more thoroughly and link some lessons from the critical moments in ProComp to a broader literature that explains how policy entrepreneurs do their work. We find remarkable resonance in portions of this framework with what Jupp, Gonring, and others did in Denver between 1998 and 2007.

Chapter 1 places ProComp in the context of other attempts to reform how teachers are paid. In chapter 2, we discuss the origins of the idea that became ProComp in Denver. Chapter 3 addresses the period of incubating the idea and moving toward a specific proposal on which the teachers and the public would eventually vote. In chapter 4, we discuss the details and challenges of the campaign to win the approval of Denver teachers. Chapter 5 focuses on the second campaign, to win support and funding from Denver taxpayers for this new initiative. Chapter 6 addresses the nuts-and-bolts implementation challenges for ProComp after it became official Denver Public School policy. In chapter 7 we examine common misconceptions about ProComp's development, as well as the real lessons the program offers others interested in PFP reform. Finally, in chapter 8 we discuss more explicit lessons that ProComp offers future education entrepreneurs.

1

ProComp History and Development

"The Nation's Most Ambitious Teacher Pay Plan"

While it has enjoyed the spotlight of national and international news, ProComp remains largely misunderstood and even misrepresented. Though easier to grasp than the federal government's prescription drug benefit plan, it is far more complex than the single salary schedule and most performance pay systems. It resists sound bites, confuses and confounds.

Later, we will present the inside story of how ProComp and its complexities came to be—bruises, blemishes, and all. And, in chapter 7 we will highlight several major misconceptions that we hear in conversations around the country about ProComp's origins and how it actually works. These fallacies range from the roles of the union, administrators, and school board in supporting the reform to how much of teachers' salaries are actually tied to student performance and other elements. Here, however, we present the thing itself, by first putting it in the context of compensation history and recent experiments and national trends in the development of pay-for-performance systems.

History of Public-Sector Employee Compensation Practices

Teachers are not the only public employees for whom it has been difficult to create appropriate salary systems. At least since the 1883 Pendleton Act's initiation of a federal civil service system in the United States, public-sector pay scales have been based mainly on a combination of an employee's initial education and training levels, job experience, and seniority. The civil service approach was developed largely in reaction to the spoils system of public employment most associated with President Jackson's tenure at the federal level and the rise of urban political machines in American cities.[1] Literally, under the spoils system, newly elected government officials rewarded their campaign supporters with well-paid government jobs without necessarily demanding an honest day's work. At the time, the U.S. Postal Service was by far the biggest government employer. Believe it or not, as many as 15,000 postal workers were replaced with each new presidential administration. Not surprisingly, the mail did not always make it to its end destination. The customer, the American public, was not satisfied.

Motivated in part by these failings and in part by their own self-interest, a coalition of business elites, good government types, and others worked to develop civil service systems, which required potential employees to demonstrate some notion of merit before obtaining a government position. Built in part upon Woodrow Wilson's idea of a split between politics and administration, in which the administration of programs would resist partisan orientation, civil service employment now had a theoretical basis, summed up in an old aphorism: "There is no Republican or Democratic way to pick up the garbage." The split was an idea for which Progressives of their time fought aggressively, although one that some scholars have subsequently debunked by pointing out that politics and administration are realistically inextricable, even in mundane areas.

Still, aided in part by an existing model of an effective civil service system in England, reformers gradually introduced civil service systems into American governments at all levels. To get most government jobs, applicants had to show a combination of educational training and success on exams relevant to expected job performance, among other criteria. Government employers based salaries on the quality of these inputs and, even more so, by time in government service, in essence rewarding workers for staying longer in their government positions. In addition to creating an input- and seniority-based compensation system, concern remained that turnover based on political affiliation would still occur.

Progressives therefore worked to grant these employees fairly strong job tenure protections, making it difficult to fire career government employees, except in the most extreme cases.

For about a century, this civil service merit system was the dominant form of public-sector employment. In the late 1970s, reform efforts emerged, engendered by the negative effects of the excesses of job-tenure systems and the absence of financial rewards for high performing employees. Under President Carter, for example, the federal government established a Senior Executive System (SES) for high-level federal officials, providing greater flexibility and the means to pay bonuses for exceptional performance. Thirty years later, the SES is not generally viewed as a great success.[2] But it did establish the concept of greater pay for top performance in government.

PFP for government employees received a boost in the 1990s with the publication of Osborne and Gaebler's pathbreaking book *Reinventing Government: How the Entrepreneurial Spirit Is Transforming the Public Sector* and the emerging concept of a "New Public Management" focused more on output and outcomes than inputs.[3] These reforms borrow from the private sector's approach of differential pay based on productivity in reaching the organization's goals. Indeed, pay for performance has been an obvious approach in many business organizations. However, even in the business sector, problems with actually implementing effective pay-for-performance solutions remain unappreciated, even at the CEO level.[4]

The movement to reinvent government along the lines of the private sector has intensified the pressure to create more flexible human resource policies in regard to initial employment, financial reward systems, and the ease with which an employer can terminate an employee for poor performance. While intellectual elites and policymakers frequently discuss these ideas, they have gained little traction in the real world of public management and employment, partly because public-sector employee unions have become the most powerful labor unions in America, and partly because the solutions are not simple.

Thus, concepts of public-sector employment have come nearly full circle in the last century. The obvious shortcoming of the spoils system led to a solution that itself created a rigid, calcified, heavily bureaucratized employment system. One hundred years later, we find ourselves criticizing the civil service system and longing for a more flexible, rewards-based public-sector employment structure. This sounds a lot like the situation in public education.

Teacher Pay

Indeed, much of the history of government employee compensation has strong parallels in public education. In fact, the widespread establishment of free public education for all American children roughly coincided with the movement toward more input- and seniority-based civil service pay structures in the United States. Not surprisingly, today the salaries of most of America's four million public school teachers are based on the degrees they hold, their additional hours of professional training and development, and the number of years they have taught children. "If you haven't died over the summer," teachers joke with morbidity but some accuracy, "you get your raise."

While some of the technical and political conditions that make PFP more promising today are new, such as No Child Left Behind (NCLB) accountability and value-added assessments of teacher quality, pay for performance itself is not a completely new concept. A small academic literature examines older experiments, most of which did not work successfully for a variety of reasons. In Texas, for instance, school districts ran into financial problems when more teachers qualified for raises than system leaders had anticipated. In Kentucky, concerns arose about cheating on tests. In other jurisdictions, pay increases tied to tests led to charges that teachers were simply "teaching to the test" or that they were engaging in unproductive competition for limited dollars.[5]

Despite an absence of success on the ground in real school districts, nearly 30 state legislatures have created policies that allow for and sometimes encourage PFP systems for teachers. Only 12 percent of districts, however, use any form of merit pay, and that pay averages only about 2 percent of teacher base salaries.[6] Most districts simply are not inspired by their state legislatures, declining to exploit laws that would allow them to move forward with compensation reform. There have been more recent attempts to somehow link teacher PFP and student learning, but most of these merit-pay programs have been abandoned or cut back quickly.

Most recently, a few states have led the charge to implement PFP plans more widely. Arizona voters passed a sales-tax increase in 2000, specifying some of the funds for support of teacher PFP plans, but little implementation has yet occurred. In 2002 Florida's state legislation directed districts to reward teachers for improved student performance, but implementation has been slow. The state government instituted policy changes in 2006 to speed up the process. However, the Florida Education Association sued the state to stop implementation in November of that year, while the United Teachers of Dade County answered with a suit of its own the following month, with this legal challenge aimed at the Miami-Dade School District. In 2007 the Florida legislature provided more flexibility to districts. Iowa instituted a pilot program in ten districts in 2002, using PFP incentives for teams of teachers within schools rather than for individual teachers. Facing a chronic problem of low teacher salaries in the state, Kentucky began a PFP plan in five districts in 2003. In 2004, with the strong support of the governor, Minnesota announced a plan to implement a version of pay for performance as a pilot program in a handful of districts, and in 2005 the legislature created a law allowing schools and districts to opt in to an alternative payment system, though few have joined in. And Governor Rick Perry of Texas recently issued an executive order to make grant funds available for 100 pilot schools to reward their best teachers, as measured by student learning. Indeed, momentum for PFP continues to build at the state level, though some wonder whether states can effectively push it from the top down, as opposed to supporting more organic bottom-up development at the district level.

A few large urban districts have also tried to implement PFP plans, but without great success. Most recently, Philadelphia and Baltimore experimented with pilot programs. Their plans proved very cumbersome and hard-to-implement, focusing more on teachers evaluating each other than on actual student outcomes and performance.

In 2000–2002, in another prominent case, teachers and their union in Cincinnati, Ohio, worked with the district to develop a PFP plan based on the development and demonstration of knowledge and skills. But the district administration acted on a too-short timetable, did not convince teachers that their evaluations would be fair, and did not do enough to convince veteran teachers that they would not actually lose salary under this plan. Thus, in May 2002, the district's teachers union voted down the plan, with 1,892 votes opposed and only 73 in favor. Teacher compensation expert Allan Odden argued: "The major reason for the defeat was in the implementation. There was not enough communication. Some issues were unresolved. . . . People were scared; if they got a lower score, they could have lost money. . . . The evaluation system is valid; it doesn't have technical flaws. It was transition and implementation issues."[7]

Cincinnati's very visible and public failure caused many in other districts to rethink the idea of making such difficult political efforts all for naught. Although the district claimed it would spend $6,000 per teacher on the new evaluation system, and evidence showed that higher teacher evaluations led to higher student outcomes, for many the Cincinnati case conclusively showed that teachers unions do not trust PFP plans.

Though Cincinnati failed to implement a districtwide plan, other major American cities are moving forward with their own efforts, many with the support of the federal government's new Teacher Incentive Fund (TIF). Along with Denver, grant recipients such as Dallas, Memphis, Houston, Chicago, and Philadelphia have plans under development. In January 2006, Houston teachers began receiving bonuses for improving student achievement, in a program that is in addition to, not in place of, the single salary schedule and which limits the number of teachers who can receive additional pay.

In contrast to the traditional advocates of pay for performance, who look to markets for their inspiration and support greater flexibility in teacher pay, Democratic presidential challenger John Kerry outlined in his 2004 election bid a plan for teacher quality that relied heavily upon federal financial incentives to expand PFP for teachers. Thus, the issue appears to be crossing over some traditional partisan boundaries, and while Democratic candidates are often said to be beholden to the positions of the national teachers unions, this was clearly not true here for Kerry.

Foundations have been increasing their support for PFP. For example, the Milken Family Foundation incorporates PFP into its Teacher Advancement Program (TAP),which has been adopted in many schools and districts, including in three schools in Cincinnati. The program provides teachers with information about multiple career paths, ongoing professional growth, instructionally focused accountability, and performance-based compensation.

Related to TAP's efforts, a growing number of politicians, policymakers, teachers, and teacher union leaders have been trying to elevate the profession so that it is perceived and compensated more like the medical and legal professions. Usually the proposals they push, however, such as the National Board for Professional Teaching Standards, involve more credentialing. In fact, pay plans that include large bonuses or permanent salary increases for National Board Certification have proliferated.

On the technical side of PFP, more governors and high-level education decision-makers have become more comfortable with longitudinal, value-added assessments of student achievement as a determinant of teacher quality. William Sanders and Sandra Horn have argued that what teachers do in the classroom is measurable; thus, rewarding teachers based on that performance is feasible.[8] While Thomas Kane and Douglas Staiger have demonstrated concerns about the short-run statistical validity of rewarding or punishing teachers based on tests in small classes and in small schools, these concerns likely can be overcome over time by adjusting the compensation stakes appropriately, as well as using a range of performance outcome measures.[9]

While there is growing proof that the quality of teaching positively affects student performance, there is as yet very limited evidence about whether financially rewarding quality teaching actually increases student performance, which is the ultimate goal of PFP plans. Data from Tennessee, which experimented with both class sizes and teacher pay plans, shows mixed evidence: students of some teachers who received incentive pay increased their achievement levels, while others did not.[10]

A new study released in January 2007, using data from many districts around the country, does show a positive relationship between teacher pay for performance and actual student performance.[11] There is also some evidence that PFP plans can help retain and attract quality teachers, which could be expected to enhance student performance in the long run.[12]

Indeed, as enhanced technical abilities collide with increased political will and are aided by grant dollars from the TIF, PFP plans do appear ready to proliferate. While hardly perfect or developed to the point where the best pay systems in the country will someday be, Denver's ProComp takes teacher compensation reform to new heights. The plan also continues to play an important role in advancing the teacher-pay debate, as ProComp leaders meet with and talk to governors, legislatures, school boards, chambers of commerce, business groups, TIF program framers and grantees, and even the president of the United States.

However, we suspect that key actors and players in and around the education system know very little about the critical elements involved in actually implementing successful PFP plans or have unreasonable expectations of linking all of teachers' salaries to student performance. Hopefully, examinations of the history of PFP, joined by an understanding of the pragmatism of ProComp as it resolves some of the technical issues of changing teacher pay, will spur future efforts or inform those reforms already underway. The practical politics of getting ProComp done will be the subject of chapters 2 through 6. Here, though, we turn to the thing itself, the complex system that endeavors to resolve a slew of technical issues, the pragmatic invention of teachers and administrators, the system that the *New York Times* called "the nation's most ambitious teacher pay plan," ProComp.[13]

The Thing Itself

Designed by a group of teachers, administrators and citizens through a deliberative process we will outline in subsequent chapters, ProComp is the result of a four-year pilot and another six months of reflection. Supported by a $25-million-per-year property-tax increase, ProComp eliminates the single salary schedule by providing teachers a menu of compensation opportunities from which to build their career earnings. It is a dynamic system in which each individual teacher is her own reference point, rather than a static one that organizes teachers into steps on a salary schedule.

ProComp is not a PFP system for purists who would reward teachers on the basis of student achievement alone; rather, it is a hybrid that incorporates a variety of outcomes that the union and the school district value: a commitment to teaching in hard-to-staff schools and assignments; a demonstration of new knowledge and skills, as well as satisfactory performance; and, most importantly, a demonstration of accurately measured student growth. As a result, ProComp has four components: student growth, market incentives, knowledge and skills, and professional evaluation.

Student-Growth Component

There are three elements of ProComp's student-growth component that combine to reward teachers with both bonuses and permanent salary increases. Under the first, student-growth objectives, teachers collaborate with their principals every year to set measurable expectations for their students. These objectives are more than a measurable finish line in the race to improve student learning; they are a roadmap for how to run the race. Principals and teachers agree on the assessment that will be used, the amount of measured learning each student will achieve, the period of time, and even the strategies the teacher will use in order to reach the objective. Further, objectives are working tools used by teachers and principals three times a year to assess student progress. If, by the end of the year, a teacher achieves both objectives, she receives a small permanent salary increase; if she achieves only one, she receives a small bonus. If she achieves neither objective, she receives no additional compensation.

DPS and DCTA view the student-growth objective-setting process, the subject of so much effort in the PFP pilot that will be described in chapter 3, as the cornerstone of ProComp, not because it is the largest potential moneymaker for a teacher but because it represents what the union and the school district consider a fundamental practice for educators. As we will discuss, the PFP pilot, and the research study that supported it, proved that when objectives are tied to compensation, teachers and principals pay much closer attention to the objectives than when there is no money attached.

In addition to this cornerstone, the student-growth component features two other elements, with the first relying on the state's standards assessment, Colorado Student Assessment Program (CSAP). Under this element, DPS and DCTA use a quasi value-added methodology to determine which teachers have extraordinary rates of student learning in their classrooms. A teacher who exceeds expectations for student growth receives a substantial sustainable increase to her pay; in other words, if a teacher achieves routine expectations for student learning, she receives no added payment. Of significant interest to the field of alternative teacher compensation, DPS and DCTA experiment with pay that can be taken away. So, if a teacher who has achieved these exceptional outcomes in some future year actually has results that fail to meet district expectations, she will lose one of the incentives she previously earned. If she meets routine expectations every year afterward, she will continue to receive it. Moreover, if a teacher works in a setting that addresses more than one state standards test, she can achieve more than one of these incentives in any given year; for example, a fourth-grade teacher, who has the important job of teaching reading, writing, and math, can receive three separate increases. Similarly a ninth-grade-language arts teacher who teaches composition to 14-year-olds may achieve two incentives, by getting exceptional results on reading and writing assessments.

The final element in the student-growth component is a fairly standard school-based incentive in which all faculty members receive bonuses at schools identified as "distinguished" using a performance metric agreed to by the district and the union. The metric identifies schools as distinguished using a basket of performance indicators, not a single measure. These include overall performance on the state standards test, change in performance from one year to another on the state assessment, and measured student growth. DPS measures student growth using a quasi value-added methodology that looks at individual student performance across two years. In addition, the distinguished-school metric includes information on parent and student satisfaction, student attendance, and improvement in student attendance.

Knowledge-and-Skills Component

The knowledge-and-skills component also contains three elements. ProComp teachers no longer receive salary increases by purchasing graduate credits. In the old system teachers were advanced on the traditional salary schedule when they received 30 and 60 hours of coursework after a bachelor's degree, a master's degree, a masters plus 30 hours, or a Ph.D. Under ProComp, the cornerstone of the knowledge-and-skills component is an incentive for completing a professional development unit (PDU).

To earn a PDU, a teacher must do more than sit through a course. The Denver program emphasizes that to earn one a teacher must also demonstrate in her classroom the knowledge and skills she has developed and reflect using data on whether the application of that knowledge and skill made a difference in student learning. When a teacher completes a PDU, she earns a modest salary increase.

Professional development units permit Denver and its teachers to move dramatically away from a dependency on higher education administration of graduate level credit toward professional development directly administered or supported by the school district. In other words, they create a way to reward teachers who rigorously apply what they have learned in job-embedded staff development. This breakthrough will allow Denver to manage instructional practice much more closely than the traditional salary schedule, which requires teachers to leave the district's professional development systems and go to a graduate credit–granting institution to get a salary increase.

This element obviously presents huge administrative challenges for a district that may some day have over 4,000 teachers earning PDUs every year. District teachers and administrators are attempting to address this administrative challenge by employing one-third of all teachers engaged in this element as peer reviewers, who in turn earn their PDUs by assisting teachers in the development of their units, checking in with their colleagues on a regular basis, and then serving on a team that will decide whether teachers have demonstrated the knowledge and skills the unit is supposed to develop.

There are two other elements to the knowledge-and-skills component. The first of these recognizes teachers who have received advanced degrees, licenses, or certificates, such as the one granted by the National Board for Professional Teaching Standards. It is important to note here that teachers who remain in the classroom do not receive a pay increase if they earn an *administrative* license, as the certification has little application to the work they will be doing with children. Under ProComp, all advanced degrees and certifications must have practical classroom applications. Also, the district and the union have agreed to grant a $1,000 tuition reimbursement account to each teacher, who may use this reimbursement to offset any professional development cost.

Market-Incentives Component

ProComp teachers also receive bonuses if they make a commitment to teach in a hard-to-serve school and/or take a hard-to-staff assignment. Under ProComp, the union and the school district annually agree on the list of assignments identified as hard-to-staff and schools identified as hard-to-serve, using different methodologies. The method used to identify hard-to-serve schools is based on the demographic profiles of the school; by relying on demographics, and not student achievement scores, ProComp avoids creating a perverse incentive that would cause teachers working in schools serving tough populations to lose their bonus if achievement improves. This approach relies on a basket of school demographic indicators that include the number of students eligible for free and reduced lunch and Medicaid, crime statistics from the neighborhoods from which students come, the percentage of students identified by the state as English-language learners, and the percentage of students who have severe and profound special education needs. As a result, there is actually a hard-to-staff school in one of Denver's most affluent neighborhoods because many children are bussed in from neighborhoods with high crime rates.

The market-incentives component is also offered to teachers who choose to fill hard-to-staff assignments. These are identified based upon two sets of data: regional surveys of the number of licensed professionals, produced by degree-granting institutions, and teacher turnover data, produced by the school district. When combined, these two sets of data provide a very different look at what hard-to-serve assignments actually are. The district has identified teachers of middle school math, English as a second language, special education supporting students with severe and profound needs, speech and language specialists, and school psychologists as hard-to-staff assignments. This conflicts with the widely held view that all secondary math or science assignments are hard to fill. By casting a wider net and looking beyond teaching assignments, the district found providers of student services were enormously difficult to find; furthermore, by studying district-turnover data, the district and the union learned that while it is hard to find teachers to fill some assignments, they actually tend to stay in those assignments once they are hired. This is the case for high school math and science teachers as well as special education instructors who teach students with mild and moderate disabilities. The assignments of greatest urgency for a school district are in fact the ones for which supply is scarce and turnover high.

Teachers in hard-to-staff schools and positions receive modest bonuses. DPS and DCTA decided not to use bonuses large enough to attract teachers from throughout the district to work in these assignments; instead they chose incentives sized to retain teachers and stabilize the rate of turnover over time.

Professional-Evaluation Component

The final component of ProComp recognizes teachers who are identified as performing at "satisfactory or better" levels, based on observed teacher performance. DPS and DCTA agreed to call this component *pro-*

fessional evaluation to reflect changes in the evaluation system that make it more rigorous and content-based across all classrooms. Under this plan, administrators evaluate performance against five standards, and, as part of this evaluation, teachers must present a body of evidence based on practice that includes student work. Teachers receive a small salary increase the year they are evaluated if their performance is satisfactory in all five areas. Because probationary teachers are evaluated annually and tenured teachers are evaluated every three years, the size of the incentive is adjusted for the frequency of the evaluation period.

It is important to note that DPS and DCTA considered and rejected paying teachers larger increases when their performance was deemed exceptionally good or distinguished. This choice was based upon experience with public- and private-sector merit-pay systems in the early 1990s, experience showing that without an extraordinary commitment to inter-rater reliability, managers tend to over-identify high performers. When DPS and DCTA looked at long-term cost projections for ProComp, they saw that the fiscal consequence of this tendency could have proved fatal. The effort to establish inter-rater reliability among people observing teacher performance would be too demanding and costly, so the parties decided to not try to identify distinguished performance.

The Opt-in Feature and Sustaining Two Systems

One principle of basic fairness agreed to by the union and school district in advancing ProComp is that no teachers would be forced into a pay system they did not want to enter; therefore, the union and district agreed that any teacher hired before the adoption of ProComp would be given seven years to decide whether to enter the new system. All teachers hired after December 31, 2005, automatically enter ProComp, however.

Current enrollment numbers have, in fact, exceeded all expectations. Over 1,600 teachers, nearly 40 percent of the workforce, are already enrolled. Some 780 signed up during the first opt-in window between November 5 and December 31, 2005, beating even the most optimistic expectations of ProComp team members in the office pool.

It is not hard to understand why so many teachers have signed up. Although the financial benefits of the new system may vary for a teacher, depending on where she is in her career, in the long run a teacher can make a lot more money under ProComp. (After all, that was the intent of creating an additional funding stream for the new system.) In fact, a middle school math teacher who completes a PDU, meets her student-growth objectives, exceeds expectations on the state standards test while working in a hard-to-staff school that becomes distinguished stands to receive an annual earning increase of over $5,000. And she can do that every year.

Imagine if she receives an advanced certificate and a satisfactory evaluation on top of it, making her raise for the year in which she completes the advanced degree as high as $9,000. Indeed, ProComp makes it possible for a teacher fresh out of college to build earnings much faster than she could if she were subject to Denver's single salary schedule, making home ownership, having a family, and even a long-term career in teaching a greater possibility. Someday in the not-so-distant future, Denver will have its first $100,000 a-year teacher. Hopefully this will make talented young men and women interested in teaching think twice before entering other professions for purely financial reasons.

The $25 million authorized by voters to pay teachers for their accomplishments is locked up in the ProComp Trust Fund. Cost-of-living adjustments and other enhancements negotiated by the board of education and the union will be applied equally to both systems, with the money for those adjustments coming from revenue sources other than the mill-levy trust fund. Finally, because teachers hired before January 1, 2006, were given a choice to opt into ProComp, DPS will maintain the single salary system until the last person in it retires or leaves the school district.

ProComp and Technical PFP Issues

As the teachers and administrators who created ProComp debated which elements should become part of the system and which should be discarded or reframed, they had to grapple with many of the tech-

nical issues other communities across the history of compensation reform have encountered in their efforts to implement PFP. We frame
these technical issues here as questions, much like those debated by
ProComp's designers.

First, should ProComp reward individual teachers for their accomplishments, or should it focus on groups of teachers or even entire
schools? Bolstered by research from the pilot program, which showed
that PFP failed to engender the damaging competition between teachers other researchers have found, the framers of ProComp designed a
system that clearly focuses on the individual, with only one of the four
components of ProComp, student growth, including any kind of group
incentive.

Second, what kinds of measurements, outcomes, or outputs should
be used to make compensation decisions? The framers of ProComp
clearly went beyond using statewide assessments, finding that the results of the state test, which in Colorado had been administered long
before NCLB, could be linked to about 35 percent of the workforce. Remember, DPS employs kindergarten and first- and second-grade teachers whose students do not take the state assessment and third-grade
teachers whose students indeed take the test, though their achievement
cannot be gauged against any previous state assessment. School districts also employ social studies, art, music, technology, and physical
education teachers; instructional coaches; business educators, psychologists, and other subgroups of teachers for whom large-scale tests do
not exist or are not commonly in use, let alone affordable.

Third, should PFP plans be mandatory for all teachers or should
teachers be allowed to opt in? ProComp would not have been politically palatable to the membership of the DCTA if it had been a require-
ment. In fact, some opponents of ProComp still argue that it should be
optional for those teachers hired after December 31, 2005. As the trend
in ProComp's early enrollment data suggests, coupling an optional system with more money provides adequate incentive for teachers to take
the plunge on their own.

Fourth, how much of a teacher's compensation should be based upon
elements of PFP? Generally, research shows that school districts across

the nation ask teachers to put very little money at risk in PFP schemes. Denver is an exception. Under the school district's old single salary schedule, about 71 percent of all dollars the district pays teachers covers their base salaries, while most of the remaining 29 percent takes care of longevity and advanced educational increments. In ProComp, 59 percent of all compensation dollars cover base pay while 41 percent is paid to teachers for outcomes that the union and school district value, including student achievement. And teachers are not entitled to that 41 percent share; in fact, it is possible for a teacher to get nothing but a cost-of-living adjustment for three years if she chooses to teach physical education in a desirable school, while never completing a professional development unit or an advanced degree or certificate. She will receive a raise in her third year only if she demonstrates satisfactory performance.

Fifth, should PFP systems be symmetric, with low-quality teachers facing pay cuts as high quality teachers receive pay increases? Over time, the framers of ProComp decided that the new system would be a tool to advance the priorities of the school district, not an instrument to punish "bad" teachers. As a result, there are no quotas in ProComp. There are no set numbers for how many teachers can complete PDUs, exceed expectations on the state assessment, or meet student-growth objectives. ProComp avoids the untenable problem of denying a successful teacher an incentive, a problem that plagues other PFP systems. The existence of the trust fund makes this possible, as it enables the district to manage occasional cost overruns that may occur when more teachers than predicted do well. The ProComp Agreement actually allows the union and district to recalibrate how much money is spent on each component and element to ensure that the fund remains solvent. For instance, if an analysis of disbursements shows that the trust fund will not remain viable at current rates of expenditure for, say, student-growth objectives, then the union and the district can reduce the size of payouts to individual teachers for this element of the student-growth component.

Finally, should PFP be funded by existing revenue streams, or should new streams be created? Although no one imagined a mill-levy tax increase when the PFP pilot began, in the end project leaders opted to create a new source of revenue for two reasons. First, by putting more money on the table for teachers, ProComp framers provided an incentive for labor to adopt PFP. Second, as ProComp was created to advance the goals of the school district, the additional funds should help attract and retain high quality teachers. By increasing pay, the theory goes, the district will increase the likelihood that its teachers will stay in DPS and that smart, talented young people and mid-career changers will seek employment in DPS, forsaking both other school districts and less exciting professions, such as law, medicine, and the professional rodeo circuit.

Answering all these questions was difficult. It took nearly two years for the task force of teachers, administrators, and citizens to finish grappling with them and create one of the most advanced teacher compensation systems in the country, the policy known as ProComp. And it is to the creation of this policy that we now turn.

2

ProComp's Origins

Making Pure Dumb Luck Work

I n any endeavor—whether philanthropy or football, policymaking or policing, school reform or school lunch-making—never underestimate the power of pure dumb luck. Never disregard the accidental intersection of someone else's agenda and your own, or the simple serendipity of sitting in the right chair in the right airport at the right time, as a fellow traveler discards his copy of the *Los Angeles Times* in the seat next to you. In a particular seat in the San Diego Airport in the fall of 1996, Phil Gonring remembers sitting, retrieving that newspaper, and finding within it an article about the unveiling of *What Matters Most,* the National Commission on Teaching for America's Future's (NCTAF) effort to rally the nation around an agenda to improve the quality of its teachers.[1]

NCTAF would eventually become a punching bag for a sector of the think-tank and academic community, which took issue with not only the report's failure to privilege alternative routes to the teaching profession but also the fact that the bulk of NCTAF commissioners came from the "education establishment," including representatives of the National Education Association (NEA), American Federation of Teachers (AFT), National Council for Accreditation of Teacher Education, teachers' colleges, and universities. As the story of ProComp's development unfolds in the coming pages, it will become clear that project leaders very early on abandoned strict adherence to the commission's 1996 recommendations for teacher compensation reform, but we feel obligated to recognize that the commission's report served as an important touchstone in the development of ProComp, especially during contract negotiations in 1999 and in the first two or three years of the pilot program. But we also feel obligated to say that ProComp project leaders aligned themselves with a quite different political machine, one that often finds itself at odds with the education establishment represented by NCTAF. They partnered with a conservative Republican governor, a former GOP party chairman and Colorado's Republican kingmaker, a man who was fond of saying that he might have been the only Republican urban superintendent in America, and a dedicated member of the Party of Lincoln who chaired Denver's Board of Education at a critical point in ProComp's development. Jupp once shook President Bush's hand, while many of his union colleagues never offered theirs. In fact Jupp was labeled "the devil" by a fellow member of the NEA.

Still, one should never underestimate the intersection of someone else's interests and one's own. What matters most is how one uses dumb luck, makes it one's own, and forges alliances with those he bumps into by accident. In 1996 in the San Diego airport, unbeknownst to Gonring, he was about to begin a decade-long journey that would collide with one that began half-heartedly in the Denver Public School system in the early 1990s but would gather momentum in part because union leadership eventually picked up its own copy of *What Matters Most*.

In fall 1996, 33 and fresh from nine years of working in public schools, Gonring had been employed by Rose Community Foundation (Rose) for a little over a month. Recovering from a three-year stint overseeing the start-up of one of the first New American School Development Corporation schools, the Rocky Mountain School of Expeditionary Learning, Gonring still had not gotten used to the gifts given him by a private-sector employer. For the first time in his working life, he had time to think. No one yelled at him. Superintendents actually returned his phone calls, and ketchup was no longer a vegetable.

Through proceeds generated by the sale of the Rose Medical Center, Rose was founded in 1995. Its founding president and CEO, Don Kortz,

ProComp Timeline

1990–1998

- 1990, 1994, and 1996—Board of Education negotiates into labor agreements the creation of blue-ribbon committees to study merit pay. Committees meet infrequently, if at all. Contract eventually calls for the creation of a $600,000 fund to reward teachers for outstanding performance. No teacher receives additional compensation.
- 1995—Rose Community Foundation (Rose) created.
- 1996—National Commission on Teaching and America's Future (NCTAF) issues report, "What Matters Most," followed by 1997's "Doing What Matters Most." Reports influence both Rose's grant-making and Denver Classroom Teacher Association's (DCTA) willingness to examine teacher-pay issues.
- 1998—Denver Public Schools (DPS) superintendent Irv Moskowitz and board member Laura Lefkowitz talk to Brad Jupp about merit-pay ideas.

1999

- Moskowitz resigns; Sharon Johnson appointed interim DPS superintendent.
- Rose convenes superintendents and union leaders to discuss teacher pay. After discussion, DCTA leaders Bruce Dickinson and Andrea Giunta express interest in working with Rose to implement pay-for-performance (PFP) pilot.
- Labor negotiations culminate in agreement to pilot PFP.
- Rose makes $90,000 grant to support pilot design.
- Community Training and Assistance Center (CTAC) retained to assist in pilot development.
- Design team established.
- Pilot begins.

2000

- Rose offers $1 million to ensure a meaningful pilot. Denver Board of Education and DCTA must agree to extend pilot from two to four years. Union quickly agrees to offer. Board of Education hesitates but eventually approves extension.
- CTAC retained to research and provide technical assistance for the pilot.
- Chip Zullinger appointed DPS superintendent.
- Rose and DCTA visit MacArthur Foundation to generate additional financial support for the pilot. No money follows.
- Zullinger's staff designates Jupp as PFP design team leader.

2001

- Becky Wissink becomes DCTA president.
- Colorado Governor Bill Owens holds press conference in favor of Denver pilot.
- Jerry Wartgow hired as DPS superintendent. Board of Education prioritizes pilot in hiring process.
- Rose makes second $1 million grant.

- Wartgow creates new organization chart, with Jupp reporting directly to him.
- CTAC releases its midterm report, which shows a link between the objective-setting process and student learning.
- Joint Task Force on Teacher Compensation (JTF) created by design team.

2002

- Daniels Fund makes first grant ($500,000) to support effort.
- The Broad Foundation makes first grant to support effort ($1 million).
- Union begins PFP communication efforts with membership. Rose backs them with $160,000 grant.
- Seminar phase of JTF's work ends; design phase begins.

2003

- Becky Wissink wins second term as DCTA president.
- JTF presents ProComp design plan to teachers and principals.
- Negotiated labor agreement freezes wages, creates problems for ProComp.
- DPS pursues tax increase that does not include dollars for teacher salaries; union does not endorse tax increase, which passes anyway.
- Les Woodward, ProComp supporter, becomes Denver Board of Education chair.

2004

- Final CTAC evaluation report of pilot issued.
- JTF finalizes specific design elements of ProComp.
- Rose commissioned poll shows only 19 percent of teachers will vote in favor of adopting new salary system.
- Rose and Broad hire political consulting firm to manage ProComp campaign within union.
- Denver mayor Hickenlooper endorses ProComp at press conference.
- DCTA teachers vote 59 percent to 41 percent in favor of ProComp.
- ProComp transition team created within DPS.
- Rose, Daniels, and Broad all make grants to support ProComp implementation.

2005

- Labor-management discord during contract negotiations nearly scuttles the ProComp election.
- Kim Ursetta elected DCTA president.
- Michael Bennet named DPS superintendent.
- Denver voters approve $25 million property tax increase annually for ProComp.
- First opt-in window completed. Over 780 teachers enroll in the new salary system.

2006

- First ProComp checks are written to teachers.
- Rose makes additional $566,000 investment to aid with implementation and evaluation.

and the foundation's trustees immediately began developing an organization they hoped would be poised for the type of bold action that would have made the hospital and foundation's namesake, General Maurice Rose, proud. The hard-charging General Rose commanded the Third Armored Division, which covered more ground in a single twenty-four hour period than any other unit in World War II. A risk-taker, Rose perished leading an attack, as his driver sped around a corner and drove into the back of a German tank, where the general was greeted with a bullet to the head.[2]

While it is doubtful that Kortz had General Rose in mind when he began hiring staff, he certainly was thinking about surrounding himself with people willing to take great risks. Kortz is a prominent commercial real-estate attorney and civic leader in Denver. He remembers how he sought to create an organization that would work innovatively: "We created an environment in which the board and particularly the staff had the ability to get out and participate in areas that could be risky—in the sense that other people hadn't been—and take chances. We wanted to do more than just responsive grant-making."[3]

Through Kortz's leadership, Rose established several Centers of Excellence, grant-making program areas that he envisioned would lead change in the Denver area. Kortz worked with his trustees to cast the program areas as businesses:

> I always wanted staff to be free to develop their own programs, to be like individual companies, so Gonring could run his own enterprise. Everyone else would have their own business too, subject to the same rules that any president would have in a company—reporting responsibilities to a board and to his or her boss. They would have the same guidelines as the head of a company, but their hands wouldn't be tied. We didn't want staff to be puppets. We wanted the best and the brightest, who would have the authority to think freely. We wanted these individuals to have the freedom to make mistakes, the freedom of choice. We believed that people tend to make the right decisions if they are talented. We couldn't let them worry about making mistakes.

Founding trustee Stephen Shogan agrees. The immediate past board chair, an attorney, and a marathoner, Shogan is also regularly voted Denver's top neurosurgeon. A member of Rose's Education Committee since its inception, he explains why Rose staff would be allowed to take advantage of accidents and take risks: "Other foundations sometimes tend to be much more prescriptive to their staffs. We wanted to give our staff much more latitude. We thought the board should set overall policy, but the staff should have the latitude to push at the margins and explore the edges. We really only wanted the staff to come back to the board and committees if they got to an uncomfortable place, a place that would require a conversation with us."[4]

Besides having time to think, Gonring was learning from Kortz, Shogan, and other trustees that he had the latitude to be inventive, take advantage of happenstance, risk, and sometimes fail. As a school leader, however, he had also grown to understand what NCTAF articulated clearly: what matters most in schools is teaching. Moreover, he was thinking that his new employer could play an important role in making teaching better, especially for low-income kids, but still had not found a framework suited for advancing a teacher-quality agenda within the foundation. The anonymous fellow in the airport, the *Los Angeles Times*, and NCTAF helped to solve that problem.

After arriving home, Gonring arranged for several NCTAF reports to be delivered to his office and used the report to work with Rose's education committee and board of trustees to develop an overall vision for the philanthropy's work in education, as well as a more immediate short-term agenda. With only about $1 million a year to spend at the time, the committee could not address all four elements of the commission's agenda. Based on reconnaissance in local school districts and meetings with teachers, the state school board and administrator associations, the Colorado's state NEA affiliate and others—in short, every member of the education establishment Rose could conjure up—the committee decided to focus on only one of the commission's planks: "the reinvention of professional development." However, Rose remained willing to entertain grant proposals that would address other components of the NCTAF agenda, including teacher compensation.

When Worlds Collide

Union leader Bruce Dickinson has been around a long time, a fact obscured by his youthful appearance, fast gait, and ability to withstand 77-hour bargaining sessions. A former semi-pro baseball player, he remains undeterred by the occasional fastball management buzzes by his ear. A veteran of three teaching strikes in three different school districts, Dickinson has been a union professional for more than 33 years, spending 18 of those as executive director for DCTA. While some suggest he is old-fashioned and a hard-liner, such assertions greatly underestimate him, for he has an almost religious commitment to democracy within his organization and an unbridled optimism stemming from his belief that teachers make a huge difference in the lives of children. Dickinson is also one of the original members of the Teacher Union Reform Network (TURN).

Founded in 1996 by progressive union leaders Adam Urbanski and Helen Bernstein, the network describes its work as a "union-led effort to restructure the nation's teacher's unions to promote reforms that will ultimately lead to better learning and high achievement for America's children."[5] While some debate whether it has made a significant impact on public education over the past decade, we should not underestimate the importance of the collision between TURN and the DCTA, and the momentum that impact created for the development of ProComp.

In the spring of 1997, Dickinson and then–DCTA president Andrea Giunta heard Linda Darling-Hammond, NCTAF's founding president, speak about the commission's recommendations at TURN's annual meeting in New York City, and she made a strong impression on them. On the airplane ride back to Denver, Dickinson remembers reading the entire NCTAF report and remarking to Giunta, "This is the only one of these reports that really makes sense to me."[6] It focused on the people he believed in most, teachers. On the remainder of the flight, Dickinson and Giunta conspired to send *What Matters Most* to all the major committees within the union, hoping to get their impressions of the document and to use it as a framework for soliciting information from members that could be used at the bargaining table

Dickinson and Giunta eventually received official blessings from all the right committees and then worked with their staff to develop a survey based on the NCTAF platform. To their credit, they did not shy away from the controversial topic of teacher pay. Dickinson recalls that the union surveyed teachers on the same topics several times over the next two or three years, even drawing out teacher perceptions on the possibility of connecting their pay to student achievement. He believes that teacher support for the prospect actually grew over time. More importantly, issuing and collecting surveys and then reporting results gave the union what Dickinson says was the cover it needed to explore teacher compensation reform when the Board of Education got serious about it. Without hesitation, Dickinson suggests that the act of surveying teachers allowed members of the negotiations team to later agree at the bargaining table to pilot pay for performance without "shooting ourselves in the foot."

Taking the school district seriously on the PFP issue was no easy matter, however. As far back as the early 1980s, various school boards supported the establishment of blue-ribbon committees to study merit pay. In fact, the Denver board negotiated such studies into 1990, 1994, and 1996 union contracts. It even anteed up over $600,000 to create a fund for individual schools to distribute awards to teachers for outstanding performance, with criteria established by site-based committees. No teacher received any of the money, however—a fact that irks Gonring to no end, given that he was a DPS teacher between 1987 and 1993 and has yet to recover financially from his decision to become an educator. Although at least one blue-ribbon panel actually issued a report, Dickinson acknowledges that he failed to put much stock into the work of any of the committees. "I wasn't paying attention," he maintains. "It seemed like more of a public relations ploy. Board members wanted to be able to say that they had tied teacher raises to performance."

It is fair to say that DPS staff also did not spend too much time thinking about teacher pay or worrying about the distribution of those funds. In fact, it took the initiative of a lone board member, Laura Lefkowitz, to turn blue ribbons into action. In 1998, she pushed Jupp, who was then a middle school teacher and the union's chief negotiator, to get the union to take some leadership on the issue and convene the committee. While it is likely, given Jupp and Lefkowitz's friendly and honest relationship, that he felt comfortable enough to respond with an expletive, suffice it to say he recalls simply suggesting to the board member that this was management's, not his, responsibility.

To her credit, Lefkowitz kept pushing. She and DPS superintendent Irv Moskowitz had been thinking about teacher-compensation reform for years. In fact, it is fair to say that the proposal eventually developed by the board grew out conversations between the superintendent and the Board of Education. Moskowitz recalls that he imagined a compensation system that was simple to understand and simple to manage, one that required teachers to set three separate objectives, not all of which pertained to student learning. One objective, could, for instance, pertain to another professional activity in which the teacher participated, such as supervising a club. He wanted to keep it simple so it was sustainable and not excessively bureaucratic. There was, at the time, no talk about tax increases or raising money to support a simple objective-setting system.[7]

Moskowitz announced his retirement before the board could bring a specific proposal to the bargaining table. Lefkowitz was left to lead the charge. Through a series of discussions, the Board of Education finalized a plan and presented it to the teachers as part of the collective bargaining process in the spring of 1999. While blue ribbon commissions had produced no proposals, the Lefkowitz-led board now confronted the union with a plan to which it would have to react.

Getting Serious about PFP

The school board now had Dickinson's full attention.

At the urging of Lefkowitz in particular, the board pushed at the bargaining table a proposal that would eliminate the traditional salary system's experience increment. A teacher would no longer receive a raise for what the cynics among us might say is simply not having died over the summer or that the more positive minded in our ranks would say is a reward for having taught successfully the previous year. Under the board's proposal, a teacher would receive her annual pay increase only if she met the specific objectives she had established in collaboration with her principal the previous year. Pay increases to successful teachers would actually be larger because funds not claimed by unsuccessful teachers would be distributed among those who met their objectives.

Dickinson, however, did not see in the board's proposal any connection whatsoever to the NCTAF recommendations. Where, for instance, was the knowledge and skills component? More egregious, however, to some, was the absence of a commitment to fairness that would transcend the boundaries of individual schools. Some teachers might, for instance, benefit from lax oversight of an overburdened or incompetent principal and write easily attainable objectives, while other, more accomplished principals would demand higher standards of their teachers. Under this scenario, it was possible for poor teaching to be rewarded with a raise, while quality work might remain unacknowledged. This was intolerable to the union and seemed likely to lead to an all-out work stoppage.

With the Board of Education holding out for the elimination of the experience component, negotiations remained at a stalemate. As teachers prepared to leave for the summer, the union called for an impasse, setting the stage for an August mediation, which would coincide with the arrival of a new superintendent, Chip Zullinger, and the return of a workforce that would have to vote on any agreement brokered during mediation.

The teachers union was not about to settle for the board's proposal. Dickinson and Giunta had set the stage for a serious discussion of compensation reform, even if they would never agree to the board's specific scheme. In fact, a very real desire to study teacher-compensation reform had begun to emerge within the union, even among the most uncompromising of members. Dickinson recalls that at its April gathering of union leaders, a "real hard-liner" stood up and said he did "not like the district's proposal one bit" but argued that the union needed to do something besides saying "no" to merit pay all the time. Perhaps, he proposed, the union should study alternative compensation and figure out once and for all if it works. Dickinson remembers several heads nodding in affirmation. With his commitment to democracy paying huge dividends here, he could go back to the bargaining table, look the board's representatives in the eyes, and say his members were willing to rethink how they were paid.

At this point, the journey begun by Gonring and Rose Community Foundation in a San Diego airport in 1996 was about to collide with the adventures of DCTA, with both parties propelled by NCTAF. By January 1999, Rose was two years into its efforts to help schools embed instructional coaching into their everyday practice and was itching for another venture. Strong stock-market performance had also increased the size of the foundation's financial corpus and therefore its grant-making budget. With two years of experience and more money under its belt, the education committee began thinking about adding a plank to its grant-making program. As Dickinson had done earlier in the year, Rose turned to *What Matters Most* for guidance.

Rose had already established that it would support teacher compensation reform. At the beginning of 1999, it had made a small grant to a school district and its local union in Denver's eastern suburbs. The grant paid for facilitation and a little bit compensation-reform guru Allan Odden's time; however, it did not result in any change to the school district's compensation system. Nevertheless, it gave Rose staff and others a chance to pick Odden's brain outside the context of the particular school district's needs and to think more broadly about compensation reform, although still limited primarily to the guidelines established by NCTAF.

As Gonring began working with his committee to extend its grant-making program into the realm of teacher pay, he was guided by his own experience and what he imagined were the boundaries of likely success. Rose, he thought, could push teacher compensation into the realm of pay for knowledge and skill and perhaps some group student-achievement goals. His thinking was guided by Odden's work, his exposure to Cincinnati's short-lived teacher career-ladder system discussed in chapter 1, and of course NCTAF. In fact, he presented a white paper to the foundation's education committee in which he argued that Rose should move beyond professional development grant-making to a focus on tewarding teachers for knowledge and skill. He cited verbatim language from the NCTAF report:

> Compensation systems should provide salary incentives for demonstrated knowledge, skill and expertise that move the mission of the school forward and reward excellent teachers for continuing to teach. . . . Rewarding teachers for deep knowledge of subject, additional knowledge in meeting special kinds of student needs, and high levels of performance measured against professional teaching standards should encourage teachers to continue to learn needed skills and enhance expertise available within schools.[8]

Now, nearly a decade after the fact, Gonring is somewhat chagrined that he failed to speak more directly to the issue of student achievement. But we also need to remember that ten years ago, when the NCTAF report was released, we were without some of the recent technical innovations that allow us to link teacher performance to student growth. Further, we were without the benefit of recent scholarship suggesting that teachers who receive National Board Certification (which measures teacher performance against professional teaching standards) do not necessarily produce better achievement results than those without certification.[9] In retrospect, however, had Gonring been more dogmatic about student achievement at the time, he likely would have driven the union away and inadvertently scuttled the venture before it began.

While there is an important distinction between NCTAF's parameters for teacher-compensation reform in its 1996 report and what ProComp became, it would be unfair to say that NCTAF's 1996 recommendations should underwhelm us. In hindsight, it is a good bit of luck for the people in Denver that NCTAF tested the waters of compensation reform, for without their recommendation to tie teacher compensation to knowledge and skills, DCTA likely never would have stuck a single toe, let alone a leg into those same waters.

As a result of his presentation of the aforementioned white paper and the subsequent deliberations it prompted, Gonring received a charge from his committee to conduct preliminary conversations with Denver metro-area union leaders, superintendents, and school board members to see if Rose could play a role in advancing teacher compensation reform. The foundation held separate luncheon meetings with each group. To put it lightly, Gonring found that pay for knowledge and skill failed to resonate with school board presidents and district superintendents. Those presidents and superintendents who considered it worthwhile to pursue changes to the system of teacher pay thought it better to hitch their wagons to student achievement than get enmeshed in measuring teachers' abilities.

Union leaders, at least those willing to consider changes, expressed the opposite opinion. Three of the unions in attendance at the Rose summer meeting expressed an interest in rewarding teachers for the development of skill and knowledge. While DCTA and two other local NEA affiliates appeared willing, the other eleven argued that large class sizes and minimal financial support for public education in Colorado would undermine any effort to talk to their members about tinkering with the existing system. Although the union leaders expressed their appreciation for lunch, they really had not prepared the way that DCTA's Dickinson and Giunta had: they had not read *What Matters Most,* nor had they surveyed their members about teacher-compensation reform. Subsequently, they were not prepared to take Rose up on its offer to help them reexamine the single salary schedule.

Indeed, by the conclusion of that summer's meeting, Dickinson and Giunta were set to huddle with Gonring. Standing by a tray of cold cuts gone warm, they discovered their shared appreciation of Linda Darling-Hammond and NCTAF. Between bites of sandwiches, they discovered their mutual interest in knowledge and skill pay. Before leaving the room, they reviewed the status of negotiations with the Board of Education and the proposal that had led to impasse. Having worked in DPS and been a former union member, Gonring commiserated with Dickinson and Giunta about whether some principals would have the requisite knowledge and skills to set objectives properly with their teachers. The three of them left the room understanding the interests of their organizations had in fact collided and that they could work together to study various ways of paying teachers. Nothing could happen, however, without a negotiated settlement that would allow such a study to take place. It was not yet clear whether the collision between the DCTA and

Rose would signify anything more than the sound and fury of a minor traffic accident.

It is important to note here that Gonring's conversations with the union had gone to far greater depth than those he had with the Board of Education or the superintendent. District leadership was, after all, in transition. It is true that as soon as a new superintendent was hired, Gonring and the Rose Education Committee immediately met with him. However, it is important and honest to point out that during the initial stages of the ProComp effort Gonring had greater trust in the direction the union wanted to go and that it is possible—in fact likely—that his background as a classroom teacher contributed to his distrust of the board's proposal. As a teacher he had had experiences with administrators who knew so little about instruction that he could not imagine them involved in setting objectives and making high-stakes compensation decisions. Further, it is also important to point out that Gonring and Jupp went through teacher education at the University of Colorado and student-taught together. As a result, while they well knew each other's blind spots and weaknesses, they trusted each other in ways that only two friends seasoned together in urban schools can. In short, Jupp's opinions weighed heavily on Gonring.

"The Nation's Most Ambitious Pay Plan"

Dickinson carried a copy of the NCTAF report to the old Burnsley Hotel, a 14-story building just across the street from district headquarters. As a union veteran, he was used to lengthy mediations, which in this case would become 72 nonstop hours. Nor were these marathons foreign to Jupp, DCTA's lead negotiator and a man whose union persona the *New York Times* deftly captured by referring to his "mix of intellect and rhetorical brass knuckles."[10] Jupp had applied those brass knuckles on many occasions.

In the early 1990s his union colleagues seemed always on the verge of striking, and they actually engaged in a five-day work stoppage in 1994. During one of the near-strike episodes, a local news station caught Jupp on camera angrily chastising Colorado's then governor, Roy Romer, before snubbing the state leader and leading his fellow union members out the door. But this was nothing compared to the time he encouraged DCTA members at yet another meeting to throw pennies at the feet of the unsuspecting governor, who had refused to press the Board of Education to increase the amount of money they were willing to devote to teacher salaries. Indeed, Jupp is not one to back down from a confrontation.

Yet on that August day in 1999, he left his brass knuckles at home, knowing his potential targets would be locked away in a separate suite and on a different floor. A mediator shuttled up and down the stairs, pushing and cajoling the sides out of impasse. In tight quarters between naps on the floor and quick peaks at the television, Jupp, Dickinson, and their colleagues offered their own proposal, which took seriously the board's determined effort to rethink teacher compensation: a two-year pilot designed to test both the board's and the union's assumptions about teacher pay. Dickinson reports that the two employees of the Colorado Education Association who had been assigned to assist DCTA in mediation paced the room. "I can't believe we're doing this. I can't believe we're doing this," Dickinson remembers they uttered one after another, shaking their heads in disbelief, like a Greek chorus in a tragedy in which everybody dies.

There were several key features to the pilot as it was proposed, modified, and agreed to by both negotiation teams and finally ratified by union membership and the Board of Education on September 11, 1999. As approved, the pilot would test three different approaches to tying teacher pay to an objective-setting process. Teacher objectives would be tied to student outcomes, and the attainment of the objectives were to be measured by student progress on standardized tests. Fifteen participant schools would be equally divided among three different approaches to the writing of objectives:

1. tied to norm referenced scores on the Iowa Test of Basic Skills;
2. tied to criterion referenced tests and other teacher created measures; and
3. tied to acquisition of knowledge and skill of the teaching and learning process.

In the pilot's first year, twelve elementary and three middle schools would participate, and high schools would be added the second year. To become a pilot school, 85 percent of a school's faculty would have to vote to participate. Providing an incentive for participation, the pilot ensured that teacher participants would be rewarded, not harmed, financially. Teachers would receive $500 the first year simply for signing up for the pilot and an additional $500 for each objective they achieved, up to two. During the second year, each participant would receive $750 for achieving each objective.

As ratified, the pilot required the creation of a four-person design team that would oversee the work, with two members appointed by the union and two by the district. Released from all other duties, design-team members would, among other tasks, pursue outside funding to pay for technical-assistance experts—which they would also have to find— and an evaluation. At the end of the two-year effort, in an election union membership would decide whether a PFP program would be implemented permanently. A positive vote would lead to a new and improved salary structure that, once implemented, would eliminate pay for experience and educational advancement as in the existing pay structure. Vertical advancement, the old experience increment, would be based on the attainment of objectives, with horizontal advancement, the education increment, centered on the acquisition of knowledge and skills. PFP in Denver had become a reality—at least as a test.

The *New York Times* drew its readers' attention to the importance of the landmark agreement the day of the teacher vote to pilot PFP: "The school teachers' union in Denver is expected on Friday to approve a plan that for the first time anywhere in the country would link teachers' raises to the performance of the students in their individual classrooms." Quoting union president Giunta, the *Times* recorded the momentous occasion: "Pay for performance based on student outcomes is totally unheard of. No one has ever done it. But we think this is a reasonable program so let's test it."[11] The *Denver Post* gave similar praise to the project the day after teachers ratified the pact, calling the pilot "the nation's most ambitious teacher pay plan linking salaries to the academic performance of students." In the same *Post* article, Becky Wissink, the union's vice president, soon-to-be design-team member and eventual union president, noted, "Denver is on the cutting edge of education reform."[12]

Whether the program was in fact a good one would soon become a matter for debate. In Gonring's opinion, it was a test the Board of Education and the union were likely to fail. In fact, he would later describe it to his trustees as an invitation for the National Education Association to send lawyers, guns, and money. As Bill Slotnik, president of Boston's Community Training and Assistance Center (CTAC), who would eventually become the lead technical assistance advisor for the project, notes, it was clear that the pilot program "did not allow the district or the union to do what they wanted to do. . . . It is a prime example of 'be careful what you agree to in the eleventh hour of contract negotiations.'"[13]

The pilot looked like a complex jumble of tasks impossible to accomplish in two years. For instance, it required the design team to help teachers determine what knowledge and skills they should develop, connect those determinations to student achievement objectives, and then use a standardized test to figure out whether the knowledge and skills resulted in student learning. Moreover, it asked teachers and principals to set objectives and potentially design their own assessments without any commitment to basic fairness. In fact, during the pilot some teachers and principals set ridiculously simple objectives while others adhered to ones that were rigorous and difficult to accomplish. Further, the pilot would, in part, rely upon an assessment, the Iowa Test of Basic Skills, that was destined to fall out of favor because of DPS's—in fact every school district in the state's—reliance on a criterion referenced test, the Colorado Student Assessment Program (CSAP) legislated long before the passage of the NCLB Act. It was hoped that the pilot would provide time-trend evidence, but there was no baseline data available and only two years of pilot data likely. Finally, the PFP pilot was to be led by four members of a design team, who were all competent and successful at what they were doing but had never overseen a multimillion dollar project of this scope and magnitude.

Indeed, it could well be argued that the pilot was trouble in the making, a potential disaster for which the Board of Education and the teachers union had committed millions of dollars in teacher bonuses over the next two years. As conceived, the pilot likely would not have provided the union and the school district with a legitimate test of teacher pay for performance.

Yet at the same time, the pilot was an amazing opportunity, a gift. Gonring even called the pilot an opportunity to "get one of the Holy Grails of education reform." Here we had a union—an urban one at that—willing to take an honest look at paying teachers differently. Further, the pilot went far beyond pay for knowledge and skills. Rather than Holy Grail, it proved to be Pandora's box, and the union demonstrated a willingness to work through the chaos it would cause. Pushing Rose and others beyond the limits of the NCTAF report, the union and Board of Education had put student achievement on the bargaining table. The flaws in the pilot paled in comparison to the opportunity. The *Denver Post* had gotten it right. This *was* the nation's most ambitious teacher pay plan.

Toward a Theory of Learning

In certain quarters of organized philanthropy a popular wisdom has emerged that foundations waste their money by investing in school districts. This thought suggests that entrenched bureaucracies and unions are focused mainly on protecting their members, not on promoting the interest of children, that they make it close to impossible to reform public education in any significant way. Further, some thinkers believe that true entrepreneurs exist only outside the established education system, where they can start and operate new and innovative schools with fewer constraints.[14]

The reality is that the daily and demanding tasks of either teaching or managing in schools squelch the impulse toward entrepreneurialism. Moreover, elected boards and superintendents with little time to make their marks on the school districts they govern or oversee believe they must act quickly, having no patience for research and development. We certainly saw this impulse as the Board of Education began to consider a pilot of pay for performance. Les Woodward, who was appointed to the Board of Education as a result of a resignation and because of his interest in reforming teacher pay, recollects that the night his colleagues agreed to the two-year pilot, many were saying that DPS had to implement a pay-for-performance plan immediately, that there could not be a pilot.[15]

While it may be a natural but unhealthy political disposition of boards of education to act with expediency, the inclination is exacerbated by the very real need to improve quickly under performing schools that are damaging the hopes and dreams of children on a daily base. Whether unhealthy or rational, the drive for expediency sometimes leads school districts to develop and adopt programs overnight. The Denver Public Schools' pilot, with its three methods of paying teachers, was conceived in a three-day non-stop bargaining session in which the participants had little sleep, no outside help, and no venture capital from the Walton Foundation. To repeat Slotnik's concern: "Beware of what you agree to in the eleventh hour of labor negotiations." We should not be surprised that the pilot had problems.

Let us also remember that teachers and administrators operate in cash-strapped environments—where they are given certain allotments of paper each semester, where everyone chips in to purchase four-dollar-a-can supermarket-brand coffee to brew in the faculty lounge each morning, and where textbooks are often 15 years old. Gonring recently asked a group of teachers to "think big" while developing a proposal they planned to submit to Rose. A few weeks later, it submitted a request for $3,800. Indeed, working on the cheap is a cultural value beaten into teachers and administrators; They do not conceive that there might be venture capital in the community.

Yet anyone who spends significant time with employees in an urban district understands that among the burned-out, unimaginative, backward-looking administrators, union leaders, and teachers—all of whom are caricatures of the problems of urban education, there are, in fact, many smart, creative, talented men and women we unjustly smear as "bureaucrats." They have passion. They have ideas. They have vision. Unlike those working in foundations and think tanks, however, they do not have the time and the resources to work magic. For them, ketchup remains a vegetable. Jupp and others who would soon be connected to the pilot had considerable creative ability, but a pilot conceived too quickly under the pressure of contract-bargaining squelched those talents.

After recovering from the intoxicating news in the *New York Times* and *Denver Post*, Jupp, Dickinson, and the Board of Education sobered up quickly. As they had many times before, they had to move without much time for deliberation. Slated to begin in just a few weeks, the pilot needed leadership. DCTA appointed Jupp and DCTA's vice president, Becky Wissink, to the design team. With two secondary school assistant principals, Shirley Scott and Pat Sandos, the district rounded out the team. They also needed to find office space and eventually decided on a room in the school district's Career Education Center—it would be two years before the project was imbued with the symbolic importance of being housed in the central administration building. While settling into their new digs, they had to find 15 schools willing to participate in the pilot by October 12, pursue outside technical assistance, and arrange for an evaluation of the two-year pilot effort.

Because he had the luxury of time, his own office, and money to spend with the oversight of a board of trustees, Gonring sat at his desk thinking about how Rose could add value to the pilot, increase the odds for success, and pave the way for the most progressive teacher-compensation system in the country. Still learning philanthropy, he was in large part running on instinct and could not articulate concisely a theory of effective grant-making. A couple of years later, he would be able to state more clearly what he was thinking and what for him would become the first principle of philanthropy: "People don't want to do what you want them to do; they want to do what they want to do." In other words, he knew he could not say to the Board of Education, design team, and superintendent that the pilot was fatally flawed, that they needed to redesign it and do it the way Rose wanted them to.

He and Jupp, however, had begun to talk about giving the design team the opportunity and resources to create a plan for the pilot. During the planning stage, they thought, the sheer magnitude of the effort would become clear and, voilà, the parties would agree, among other things, that the timeline for the effort would have to be extended. Moreover the idea for an extension would be their own! As an insurance policy, however, Gonring conceived of a national "critical friends" panel of outside experts that would review the plan after it was completed and, as he imagined, tell the press, the Board of Education, and the broader community that the pilot would have to be extended. The board, therefore, would not possibly go ahead with a two-year effort because, well, they would be swimming upstream against a current of popular opinion.

The Rose Education Committee began talking about supporting such a planning effort. After a meeting between the committee, the design team and Superintendent Zullinger, on October 19, Rose awarded the district and union a $90,000 planning grant, which, as conceived, would give the parties the outside help they needed to plan the effort by paying for technical assistance, communications, and the critical friends panel which would evaluate and suggest revisions to the plan before it was implemented. In an internal document addressed to the education committee, Gonring wrote, "The two-year time frame for the project is far too ambitious. . . . Nevertheless, it is fairly certain that during Phase One (the planning stage) of the project, the time frame will come under the scrutiny of the critical friends panel and the board of education."[16]

From the beginning, although Rose was clear that it wanted any new system to acknowledge and reward quality teaching, it did not have a strong preference for what a new compensation system should look like. However, Rose did believe that that the learning induced by the grant, its provision of time and resources, would trump the school district's innate drive for expediency. It also believed that the planning stage would and should result in a second proposal to support what it imagined would be a lengthy stage two for the project.

With the planning grant approved October 19 and the clock running down on what now would be only a 19-month pilot, Jupp and his team looked for an organization that would help them develop a plan. There was no time for a traditional request for proposals, only a few days for a handful of phone calls. Jupp called university professors, think tanks, regional education laboratories, and nonprofits. Based upon his review of successful program-evaluation work the organization had done for DPS, Jupp decided to call Slotnik at CTAC. He and his staff had experience with student-achievement studies and community decisionmaking, as well as some limited experience with administrative PFP plans in Cleveland. Slotnik's organization conducted an evaluation of Denver's school-based collaborative decisionmaking bodies in the mid 1990s and knew the district and several central office staff fairly well.

In the end, Jupp and his colleagues selected CTAC as the provider because it could take on the breadth of issues raised by the pilot—they were willing to go beyond traditional education research topics—such as the effectiveness of large-scale assessments and teacher evaluation—to an investigation of school- and district-level system issues, such as the alignment of curriculum, instruction, professional development and other aspects of administration. It was Slotnik's job to help the design team build the pilot, which, like an airplane, was speeding down a runway. Over the next few weeks, he and his staff tried to coordinate the vision of DCTA and the Board of Education, while developing the technical requirements necessary to both perform a quality pilot study and incorporate ongoing evaluation.

The investment in Slotnik paid off quickly: he immediately saw that the pilot was in trouble and that it needed more focus on the link between teacher earning and student learning. In particular, he realized that, to avoid past failures, the pilot needed to be about more than financial incentives, it had to avoid being mostly punitive toward teachers, and it required major changes in thinking. Slotnik notes: "From our experience with administrative PFP in Cleveland, we knew that how you do it is as important as what you actually do."

Through his efforts, it became clear to the design team that it had been given an impossible task and that it needed more than 19 months to run a legitimate experiment. CTAC also was able to help guide the design team through planning for a major project, something these inexperienced leaders had never done before. As a leader, and as the person the superintendent would ultimately anoint as the de facto head of the entire effort, Jupp had to learn his role quickly, and through sage advice of a program officer of another foundation, Jupp was also about to provide the project with the verbal clarity it needed.

As the PFP plane sped forward, Gonring arranged for Zullinger, Jupp, and Sandos to fly on a non-metaphoric airplane to Chicago, where they met with the MacArthur Foundation and one of its program officers, Peter Martinez. Gonring and Martinez knew each other from an affinity group of education grant-makers, and Gonring had called the MacArthur employee to help him brainstorm about likely national funders for the Denver project. After suggesting some names, Martinez called back a few hours later to say that he would like to see a funding collaborative that included the Chicago-based foundation.

While, much to Martinez's chagrin, the Denver contingent failed to return home with the hope that MacArthur would fund the pilot, the trip did set the stage for a future meeting between Jupp and Martinez in a Cincinnati restaurant during the course of another TURN conference. There Jupp downed a bottle of Budweiser—he still enjoys union beer—and filled Martinez in on the details of the Denver effort. Martinez listened intently to Jupp's description of the pilot challenges and then clarified what would need to happen in Denver: "What you need is a theory of learning." The program officer's words are simple, and we would think they would be obvious to people who work in schools, whose product is in fact learning. Yet outside hardcore professional development circles, school districts tend to think of learning as something reserved for children only. However, ongoing learning is crucial to the work of adults in many professions. Scientists, for example, gain knowledge through trial and error. As we all know from watching crash-test-dummy commercials on television, automakers learn to improve their cars by analyzing the results of collisions. Software companies employ testers to find the flaws in their products so that they can improve them before going to market. Theories of learning and sets of practices to support them are cornerstones of almost every industry, yet they are often surprisingly foreign to education.

Jupp left the TURN meeting thinking like a tester of crash-test dummies, believing that the most important thing he could do would be to

make sure that the pilot would provide opportunities for the bureaucrats, the teachers and the philanthropies to act like entrepreneurs in
any other profession. A pilot could not test just one set of assumptions;
its implementers had to allow time to test other assumptions if the first
ones were not correct.

Gonring's instincts, Jupp's epiphany, and Slotnik's experience were
all coalescing toward a commitment to what Martinez articulated better than anyone else. The anchor of the Denver pilot would have to be a
dedication to the same sort of learning process seen in the best of classrooms. The pilot would have to have built into it an interim assessment
that would allow for the possibility of revision before the union and district could legitimately design a new system. As every teacher knows,
however, one cannot rush learning. A first-grade student cannot become
a twelfth-grade reader overnight, yet in a way this is what the design
team was being asked to do.

The design team now had other ideas, and, with CTAC's help, it was
ready to submit a project plan to the Board of Education and the union's
Board of Directors, a plan that would call for a four-year, $10.9 million
pilot, $5.1 million of which would have to come from philanthropy. The
first week of January, the design team presented Rose a request for $1
million, enough to cover a little over one year of the four-year effort, in
advance of its presentation to the board. At this point, the union had
no qualms about extending the pilot, although the prospect had not
been submitted to a formal vote of the members. Dickinson remembers
that the union could easily agree to the extension because he and the
president had made promises to teachers to have a legitimate research-
based study. His recollection is that CTAC played an important role in
the union's decision: "CTAC said you can't get there in two years, if the
chief researcher says that you can't do it, then you can't do it." Slotnik
agrees: "It would have been a major failure at less than two years."

The Board of Education, however, turned ashen-faced when it listened to CTAC recommend the pilot's extension and knew that the costs
would escalate accordingly. Woodward remembers the CTAC presentation and the hour-long mostly negative discussion that followed. "There
were a couple of people really concerned that the board was being ma-

nipulated by this Cambridge outfit," Woodward recalls. Slotnik believes that the case for building stronger capacity in the pilot was pretty clear and necessary, especially with the lack of baseline data and the short timeframe provided. He was confident that all of the key players "would show courage moving forward with all parts of this process." Still, all bets were off. No one knew whether the board would buy into the theory of learning.

On the Brink of Disaster

As the union and school-district boards contemplated the pilot's extension, Rose's staff and education committee reviewed the school district's plan and grant proposal, which sought funds to support CTAC's continued participation as technical-assistance provider and researcher. A number of issues loomed large, one being that at this point there were no other foundations willing to put a dime into the project. Another was what board members thought was the inherent risk of working with teacher unions. Further, the inexperience of the design team disquieted some. Finally, there was the nagging issue of the short timeline and staff's worry that the Board of Education really was not willing to extend the pilot.

In the end, however, Rose's board of trustees decided, remarkably, to make the second largest grant in the foundation's history, $1.04 million, to support an effort that addressed a key Rose priority, teacher quality, and a big idea whose time had come, paying teachers for performance. The trustees understood that they were taking a big risk; nevertheless, they believed it was indeed possible that the risk would pay off in a big way with one of the most progressive teacher compensation systems in the country. Shogan believes the foundation would approach the project entirely differently today. "We were inexperienced," he now observes. However, his pride still shines as he recalls that his decision to back the grant had concerned the board's belief that the foundation, unlike the hospital many of the board members had recently overseen, should be able to take risks. "We could become social entrepreneurs and try a lot of different things—even if they failed," he remembers. This was founding CEO Kortz's vision coming to fruition. While Rose's staff and board were inexperienced social entrepreneurs, they understood that social change is a lot like change in the business world: without great risk, there can be no great reward.

Neither staff nor the board of trustees, however, was willing to wager a $1 million investment on what had really become an 18-month pilot, so they made the grant contingent on extending the pilot to four years. The day after the board meeting, Sheila Bugdanowitz, the foundation's newly minted president and CEO, mailed letters announcing the grant and its contingency to the Board of Education, superintendent, and union president. Trying to lighten the impact she knew the demand for extension would have on board members, she thanked them and their union colleagues for the courage demonstrated in their willingness to pilot PFP. She also, however, reminded them that Rose itself was taking a great risk: "The Foundation believes that a pilot of the highest possible quality will have the greatest chance of leading to permanent implementation. . . . Consequently, Rose Community Foundation's Trustees are asking the Board of Education to take some additional steps to ensure that the pilot will be of the greatest possible quality." The biggest step would be the board's willingness to extend the pilot to four years. "Unless these steps are taken, we will, regrettably, not be able to make the grant," her letter ominously concludes.[17]

Gonring remembers receiving an angry phone call, in which she labeled Rose's tactics heavy-handed, from a board member who had just gotten on a plane and read the letter. A few days later, however, the foundation would make some members of the Board of Education even angrier. Fearing that the board would ultimately fail to extend the pilot and that an amazing opportunity to reform teacher compensation in an urban school district would be lost, Rose decided to pressure the board through the newspapers. The first principle of philanthropy ("People don't want to do what you want them to do") sometimes can be violated by a core principle of urban public education—which Gonring once overheard in a conversation among community organizers— "School districts don't change because they see the light; they change because they feel the heat."

In early February, Rose issued a press release announcing both the million dollar grant and the contingency requiring the extension to four years, hoping that the Board of Education would feel a little heat. Gonring vividly remembers the call he got from one of the *Rocky Mountain News*'s education beat writers. The reporter asked him how he thought the district would react to blackmail. While a review of the newspaper articles the following day reveals that Gonring effectively dodged the question, one board member vocalized his frustrations: "I never like to feel I'm pressured to accept anything under conditions."[18] In the *Denver Post*, the city's other daily, the same board member made his position even more clear: "I have to be convinced as to why that much time is necessary." He continued, "From the previous presentation, I wasn't convinced. A million dollars won't change my mind on that."[19]

School board members Les Woodward and Elaine Berman reacted differently. Before her election to the Board of Education, Berman had worked as a program officer at Denver's Piton Foundation and in that role had partnered with Gonring in a handful of philanthropic ventures. Perhaps it was Berman's familiarity with Gonring, Rose, and philanthropy in general, or perhaps it was her natural political instincts that caused her to speak positively about Rose's offer. "I'm thrilled an institution as highly respected as the Rose Foundation has the confidence in DPS," she told the *Rocky Mountain News*'s reporter. Woodward told the same newsman that he wanted to think about the proposal on its merits, not the million dollars; however, he added that "it's stupid to say it doesn't influence me. It affects me that they think it's worth $1 million."[20]

The Board of Education likely had many reasons to demure in the face of Rose's offer. While Woodward reports that some personal issues played out in the Board of Education discussions, the board largely faced pragmatic challenges. For one, Woodward recollects that board members had real ownership of the original plan as it had been proposed to the union at the start of negotiations. In fact, "one board member was resentful toward anything that would dilute and change it," he reports. Berman reminds us that the board had to make a serious decision about the expenditure of taxpayer funds. After all, doubling the length of the pilot would mean the district would have to double the cost of paying bonuses and design-team salaries at a time when the board confronted serious budget shortfalls. Berman believes that at the heart of some of her colleagues' unwillingness to increase the length of the pilot was pressure from senior staff, a group, she says, that was not enthusiastic about the pilot. "Staff would talk to board members and say this whole thing is a joke. Nothing's going to come of it. We're just spending a lot of money, money that we desperately need, and we're doing it because this outside foundation wants it to happen."[21] Woodward states clearly that at least one board member was concerned about "being managed by a bunch of philanthropists" and that the board was giving up its "prerogative to tell the world what to do to somebody else."

The final vote was held in executive session. We know only that the board voted to extend the pilot, although there is certainly a hint that the vote was not unanimous. Woodward reports that the conversation was tenuous but that what really changed his mind was Slotnik's insistence that the group "couldn't have a legitimate study, the kind of data that would be valid in any way" without a four-year effort. Indecisive board members ultimately decided, as Woodward recalls, that without the money, "we probably did not have the wherewithal to conduct anything like a reasonable evaluation of what was going on, and we really needed that if we were ever going to convince the union to go forward" with a new compensation plan.

The next day the papers reported the extension, but neither mentioned the tactic employed by Rose. The following Saturday, however, the masthead editorial in the *Rocky Mountain News* carried the headline, "Rescuing Performance Pay." It articulated the case for extension better than Rose could have hoped by pointing to the complexity of the pilot and the difficulties the union and district encountered in launching the effort. The editorial concludes that two years would not be enough:

> It's not a fair test of the pay-for-performance concept, and increasingly there's been talk that the pilot would need to be extended in order to provide convincing results when the teachers eventually vote on whether to make the pay-for performance plan policy for the entire district. The sticking point, not surprisingly, was cash.

During the pilot, the bonus money is in addition to whatever raises teachers would normally get under their current contract for longer seniority or better credentials. The district committed $2.8 million for two years. But each additional year could cost up to $1.5 million, and that situation posed an uncomfortable choice for the board. Either it would have to spend more than it really wanted to, or it risked wasting what it had agreed to spend on an inconclusive result.

Rose's $1 million offer made the choice at least a little easier.[22]

Although the newspaper downplayed Rose's aggressive approach to philanthropy, we should not dismiss the maneuver without critique. Did the foundation go too far in pushing a publicly elected board to change policy and spend taxpayer dollars on an extended pilot? Certainly Rose's tactic is within the bounds of what is allowed by law for community foundations, public charities not subject to the same rules around lobbying that, for instance, private philanthropies are. Further, we could argue that an important role philanthropy plays is to push institutions, even government institutions, to perform more effectively for the public good. This, in fact, is what the foundation strove to do by suggesting that the school district could not produce a quality product for the Denver community unless it gave the pilot more time.

Rose never demanded that the Board of Education and the union develop a specific compensation system. The foundation suggested merely that the Board of Education, district staff, and teachers could better address an important issue of public policy through an extensive period of study. Patience is a luxury that foundations have and the value they potentially add to public policy creation. Rose, unlike members of the Board of Education, was not confined to the time constraints placed on public officials as a consequence of term limits and could take the long view in the development of teacher pay policy. It did not have to rush to judgment before its term expired.

Moreover, it is certainly fair to say that the Board of Education struck the largest and most influential policy blows in the early stages of the ProComp effort. By insisting that the pilot examine the connection between teacher pay and student achievement, the board ensured that more than pay for knowledge and skills would be on the table. Without

Lefkowitz nudging Jupp and then the entire union, the pilot would not have occurred in the first place.

In short, a blizzard of phenomenon harnessed in February of 2000 is the story here, not a single act. While Rose's tactic may have paved the way for a successful pilot, ProComp never would have been given a shot without the chance collisions of NCTAF, the *Los Angeles Times*, TURN, Martinez of the MacArthur Foundation, Lefkowitz, Jupp, the Board of Education, Moskowitz, Berman, Woodward, Dickinson, and a union prepared to lead a pilot where no NEA affiliate had dared tread before. Nor would it have happened without the workmanlike innovation and improvisation that took those collisions as they came and adjusted expectations as necessary. With adequate time and resources, the board and the union now had a chance to develop what the media had called "the nation's most ambitious pay plan."

3

The Skunk Works

"Who the Hell Is Supervising You, Anyway?"

Given the hullabaloo surrounding the decision to extend the PFP pilot, few would have expected it to become a marginal enterprise operating on the fringe of the district within DPS. The board of education's fiery two-month debate over the time extension led many to conclude that the effort to transform teacher pay was central to DPS's policy efforts. The coming months would instead demonstrate minimal organizational focus as the board of education moved from one topic to another in turbulent waters churned by superintendent turnover. The board's counterparts within the union remained swamped with day-to-day work, which was punctuated by contentious debates at the bargaining table over miniscule differences in real compensation.

As a result, district administration just added the PFP effort to its longer list of loosely strung together initiatives. Greater direction would come in 2001, when the board of education hired Jerry Wartgow as superintendent, but during the entire period of the pilot it would be hard for anyone in Denver to think of the PFP pilot as the major policy initiative it would eventually become. Although the neglect did not feel very good to PFP leaders at the time, it begs an important question: was it necessarily a bad thing?

February 2000 Optimism

Looking back at the PFP pilot, we could easily see February 2000 as not only a high point but also, at least potentially, the beginning of a renaissance for DPS. Headed by a new superintendent, the district had just made a joint commitment with the teachers union to extend the pilot two more years, granting the project time to develop credible recommendations. All seven board members were squarely behind PFP as a policy concept, even if two or three were dyspeptic following the board's decision to grant the project more time. The project was fully staffed; its design team of two teachers and two administrators occupied a bullpen office in one of the best schools in the city. The team's collaborative structure marked a tentative and hopeful commitment to a labor-management partnership on one of the toughest policy issues in the country. The district made a significant financial commitment, establishing a budget that covered design team salaries, ample supplies, and millions of dollars in teacher bonuses for the duration of the pilot. Twelve elementary schools and a middle school had answered the call and agreed to participate in the pilot earlier that fall—not quite the 17 schools imagined by DPS and DCTA when they agreed to enter the pilot, but at least a balanced group of elementary schools. Now that the pilot had been extended, it was the perfect foundation for the upcoming four-year study, and there would be time to draw additional schools into the project while supporting the 13 original pilot members.

Even better, the project had just received $1 million from Rose, which created a second and important surge of attention and energy for the effort, raising expectations that more philanthropic revenue could be raised in the future. Now, with some of the funding necessary to pay for technical assistance and ongoing research, the design team worked to cultivate a more detailed version of the project plan they had developed in the fall of 1999. They envisioned the pilot as more than an interesting, though isolated, social science experiment. They conceived of the pilot as an effort to establish the capacities within the district and union to implement a PFP program districtwide, if the research study ultimately generated positive findings and the board and union voted to adopt a new salary system.

While it had begun with a grant from Rose in 1999, the new grant cemented the relationship between the PFP pilot and the Community Training and Assistance Center (CTAC), the organization, led by Bill Slotnik, that now would conduct the evaluation over the life of the pilot and provide technical assistance to the design team. Understanding that the organization would lend great credibility to the project, union leaders Becky Wissink and Brad Jupp strongly endorsed CTAC's deep involvement in the project. They recognized the legitimate depth of focus CTAC would bring to work that required an exploration of the substructures beneath teacher pay. CTAC understood, they thought, the practical implications of a districtwide PFP program as well as the broader regional and national policy implications of the project. Therefore, Wissink and Jupp were simply able to fob off some of the controversy of the pilot within the union by saying, "Look, CTAC is conducting an important study of a policy issue that isn't going away."

While board members and administrators may have been more skeptical of CTAC's role than the union at this point, CTAC's involvement added the outside authority and integrity necessary to make the pilot credible. In short, the pilot could not be perceived as an inside job that the district and the board were trying to ram down the throat of union leaders. To further bolster the pilot's credibility, Rose agreed to serve as the fiscal agent for all grant funds received over the life of the pilot and to contract directly with third-party providers, including the researchers. If DPS had contracted directly with CTAC, teachers might argue that the results of the research study had been cooked and paid for.

While CTAC would not provide technical assistance over the full course of the four years that the organization would be conducting the research study, at this pivotal moment its technical assistance was invaluable. Not only did the CTAC provide greater credibility for the project, but it also expected more from DPS and DCTA than, in hindsight, they did of themselves. CTAC's staff expected a structured project with a clear purpose, not an improvised one. As Slotnik notes, DPS initially had a "let one thousand flowers bloom" approach to the pilot, which he saw as simply too unstructured.[1]

CTAC expected aligned support from the board to the superintendent to the administrative staff in the district's central office. It also expected the design team to tow considerable organizational weight within DPS. And it provided the type of managerial experience that no one on the design team yet had; Slotnik recalls that CTAC often raised new ideas, which were often met with knee-jerk *nos* initially, then were later successfully adopted as part of the process. Six months into the project, CTAC had become a substantial asset.

We might conclude that all the conditions for pilot success were set, but, in fact, from February 2000 through the end of 2003—when the design team brought forward to teachers and the public the final product of the pilot, a recommendation for a new teacher compensation system— the PFP pilot may be characterized best as having been cut loose almost entirely from DPS, DCTA, and the public at large. While no one would have said that transforming teacher pay was not a priority in DPS, pilot advocates certainly contended that at any given moment there were always other, higher priorities.

During this period, the design team was left to its own devices, isolated in large part from the main work and direction of DPS and, perhaps for the better, cut off from the persistent tumult, coming from all angles, that often undermined the district's ability to establish a durable direction. Colorado's accountability laws were changing along with the rest of the country's, with standards, assessments, and public reporting of school performance; the board of education had to find a superintendent it could depend on; district administrators remained in limbo, waiting until the board selected a new leader who would set direction; the union continued to scrap for pay increases and hold tight to work rules and other contract provisions. But there were other, more specific, issues with which PFP supporters would have to contend.

Other Priorities

After signing off on the pilot's extension, the board of education moved on to other issues, many of which were driven by state policy discussions. Elected in 1998, Governor Bill Owens immediately pushed for and won legislation that created one of the nation's toughest school testing and accountability laws, well before federal NCLB legislation. As a result, the board of education, overseeing some of the state's lowest-performing schools, had to prepare for the likelihood that some of them by law would be converted to charter schools if they were judged unsatisfactory for three consecutive years of testing.

In another legislative session, Republican lawmakers introduced a voucher bill that divided the board of education, as many in its ranks feared they had to walk a tightrope. Some did not want to alienate the Republican interests that controlled both the purse strings and the direction of public education in Colorado. At the same time, they did not want to lose the revenue that a voucher law would redirect toward private schools. While the bill passed both houses of the legislature and was signed by the governor, the Colorado courts eventually declared it unconstitutional, saving the district some cash, but failing to reimburse the board for time and energy lost debating the issue.

And, as happens in most urban school districts, the board and the superintendent became distracted by a host of non-policy issues as well. Local media frequently focused heir attention on whatever the crisis de jour at the time happened to be. While these were serious issues, they diverted the board's attention away from a persistent focus on quality instruction, of which PFP was a part. In one week, the board would have to focus on the fallout from student caught sexually harassing a classmate. In another, it was a teacher accused of sexual misconduct. And during still another, the board was occupied with a child abduction outside a district school. There was even a flap over a Mexican flag that had been displayed in one of the district's high schools. The board responded as politicians do at any level of government: they put the key policy issues aside and focused on the crisis.

Yet the DPS central office staff paid little attention to the pilot either, regarding it mainly as a flawed idea, a distraction from their important work. As we have already seen, there had been a broader pattern of ignoring PFP and letting the issue disappear. Three times in the 1990s, collective bargaining agreements requiring study committees to take a closer look at new ways of paying teachers had been ignored, until board member Laura Lefkowitz finally stuck with the issue in 1998. Many administrators had once been teachers themselves and likely were not fond of the idea of PFP, holding both romantic visions of the non-financial incentives that motivate teachers and pragmatic views about the difficulty of measuring teacher performance with any accuracy. Others saw the pilot as something that was never intended to be, and especially with the extension, as having gone far beyond the original vision of the board of education.

In fact, when the board hired Wartgow in 2001, it was hard to find anyone in the central office who could be called a soldier in the army of pay for performance. Wartgow recalls what it was like: "I don't know if there was a single person in the cabinet or anyone in top administration who bought into pay for performance, and that's putting it lightly. They saw it as a distraction from what they were trying to do to survive. To them it was a huge money-soaking operation on the side."[2]

Wartgow also remembers that central administrators were critical of the design team and protective of their own work in other areas of administration. He often heard comments like: "Just because they [the design team] don't have anything else to do, doesn't mean I don't."

While Wartgow would take clear steps to prioritize the PFP pilot and eventually ProComp, it would be inaccurate to say that the inertia in quadrants of central administration completely disappeared. Throughout the life of the pilot, the design team often struggled to get what it needed. For instance, as early as October of 2000, the union president and members of the design team explained to the board of education that they needed help supporting the objective-setting process and asked the board at a public meeting for end-of-course assessments for secondary school teachers. Yet, the effort to develop these assessments did not in fact begin until 2004.

Jupp remembers that it was often difficult to get meetings with district staff overseeing instruction, that when the meetings occurred it was difficult to get decisions made, and that when decisions were made it was often difficult to get follow-through to implement these decisions in schools. Slotnik agrees that DPS top management people, especially on the instructional side, were mostly not paying close attention to the pilot, and Phil Gonring was frustrated that representatives from curriculum and instruction rarely attended leadership team meetings.

Confusion about the pilot was widespread in the beginning. Slotnik recalls a spring 2000 a Board of Education meeting where he suggested that no one understood clearly the purpose of the pilot, to which one board member responded by pounding his fist on the table and asking, "Are you saying no one in the schools knows the purpose of the pilot?" After Slotnik replied affirmatively to the question, the board agreed to a retreat process in which participants finally determined that the design team (and later the Joint Task Force on Teacher Compensation [JTF]) would be able to act on learning engendered by pilot with the hope of achieving meaningful long-term change. In addition, CTAC started writing "management letters" to the superintendent and the union leadership to overcome Slotnik's concerns that "the forces of misinformation are more powerful than the forces of information."

Like the board and staff, the union struggled to focus its members on the pilot, constantly ramping up for annual negotiations, working through grievances, and solving problems between teachers and principals. That the pilot operated ultimately in only 16 schools presented a huge communication problem, as teachers in over 120 schools remained completely untouched by this policy initiative. Rose consistently asked the union and the school district to address this challenge, since a lack of knowledge and familiarity would almost certainly torpedo the pending vote on the new system. As a result, Rose made a grant to the union to gather information about the problem. After conducting focus groups and surveying 100 teachers in the summer of 2002, DCTA found frequent misunderstandings and widespread rumors in the non-pilot schools, teachers who had tuned out PFP completely, and principals who did not believe it was their responsibility to communicate with teachers about the pilot. Some DCTA members did not even realize that they eventually would be voting for or against a proposed compensation system. In essence, most teachers remained in the dark about the PFP pilot.

Trying to Ensure ProComp's Success

Throughout the pilot, Gonring and Rose's education committee expressed concerns that neglect could be the death of PFP in Denver. Rose was in a spot that made it difficult to hold the school district accountable for deliverables. While it would have been easy to hold the third-party providers to task for their work through a contractual relationship, it was difficult to have a similar relationship with the school district for two reasons. First, no money changed hands between DPS and Rose— the foundation had contracts with nonprofits serving the pilot. Second, because the project unfolded at a rapid pace within a political context, the district, the union, and the philanthropy were literally building an airplane in midair. No one was sure what the deliverables should be. Much later in the project, as the district began implementing ProComp, Rose would make grants directly to DPS. It easily built and enforced a system of accountability, as it could withhold grant funds for salaried positions if deliverables were not met, and the school district's budget director could tell any laggards that if they did not get their work done, the district would not be able to make payroll.

So while traditional systems of accountability could not be enforced, the foundation used other tactics to get the parties to focus their attention on the pilot. At one point early in the effort, Rose convinced Governor Owens to hold a press conference. At a middle school, the governor, covered by print and television media, told an audience of school board members, district administrators, and union leaders how important the pilot was to the state and the nation. He congratulated the Board of Education and DCTA for their courage and foresight. While some thought Gonring crazy for orchestrating the event—they were skeptical about how a Republican governor big on accountability and no friend of labor could help propel the project forward—he felt vindicated after one of the more skeptical members of the Board of Education told him, "I had forgotten how important this effort is." Gonring hoped that the media coverage would make the point clear.

At another moment during the pilot, Rose called on its then board chair, Steve Farber, to meet with the DPS superintendent and board chair to remind them how important PFP was to the foundation and to

Denver. At other times, Gonring would talk directly to the current superintendent about the inertia he perceived in certain quadrants of the school district. At times, the conversations became heated as the program officer was reminded about the number of staff actually engaged in a project that would very likely result in nothing when the union voted it down.

Slotnik believes that Rose's willingness to hold up "an honest mirror" of evaluation was critical to maintaining PFP momentum in Denver during this period. He jokes that the foundation's willingness to engage in the pilot learning along with the union, DPS, and the board ran counter to his usual belief about self-absorbed philanthropy—"When someone moves into a foundation job, their IQ goes up about 50 points."

Higher intelligence or not, perhaps the most important tactic employed by Rose was proposed by education committee member and Rose trustee Al Yates, who at the time was the president of Colorado State University. He suggested that the foundation contract with someone to serve as a liaison between Rose and the school district, someone who would be seen as removed from the foundation and as a result able to push a little harder within the system. Rose eventually contracted with Cal Frazier, now deceased, Colorado's former commissioner of education, a man who had become widely regarded as the state's "elder statesman for public education. Frazier provided the design team with invaluable wisdom and advice on how to make the bureaucracy responsive. He also frequently met with the DPS superintendent and central staff to run interference for the team.

Even in hindsight, it is hard to say whether any of these interventions made a difference in the minds and behavior of central office administration. It is not just today that few people remember these interventions; even at that time most administrators had neither the time nor the inclination to pay prolonged attention. Instructional administration was reorganized twice during this period, when they were absorbed in standards-based reform and the introduction of managed instructional approaches. Operations administrators, who under Wartgow were the pilot's biggest supporters, had their time substantially absorbed by ever-growing DPS fiscal problems.

While constantly employing tactics to get the school district to elevate the pilot's status, Rose also focused on raising awareness of the project within the union. After holding several meetings to discuss the issue, Rose made a small grant to DCTA to develop a plan to raise awareness. Once the union produced the plan, the Rose board approved a $168,000 grant to support it. The 21-month communication effort aimed to inform the electorate for the impending PFP vote and was to rely heavily on face-to-face interactions between teachers.

The plan envisioned two separate human communication delivery systems, an Awareness Cadre and a Compensation Council. Designed to prepare 24 teachers to communicate with their colleagues, awareness cadre members were trained to communicate with teachers about PFP and other DPS instructional initiatives. If PFP were not couched in the context of other programs, teachers might, the union suggested, believe they were having PFP stuffed down their throats. The compensation council, on the other hand, was designed to communicate expressly about PFP to the membership. Composed of one representative from each school, the council would provide opportunities for teachers to explore the knowledge generated by the pilot and to discuss whether that knowledge supported rethinking the way teachers would be paid.

Gonring found the Rose board's decision heartening, believing that it had done the right thing to give the union a chance to communicate with its members. It was a smart proposal, he thought. In every school, teachers trained in the intricacies of PFP effort would lead informed conversations about the pilot and the compensation system that would eventually grow from it. The effort would overcome what he perceived as the pilot's most glaring weakness, the fact that the district did not regard it as a signature initiative and that therefore, besides a handful of intimates, few people knew or cared much about it. Knowledge generated by the process would create smart and informed teachers who would never vote against the amazing new salary system that would follow. While this effort hardly worked as planned, at the time Rose believed it had done what it could to ensure that information on the pilot and changes to the salary system would penetrate even nonpilot schools.

So, while Rose tried to mitigate the challenges presented by the union and the school district, it also worked to raise the status of ProComp within the philanthropic community. Project leaders needed to raise an additional $3 million, so Gonring organized the trip to the MacArthur Foundation. Early on, several local philanthropies made grants ranging in size from $10,000 to $100,000. These included the Denver Foundation, the Piton Foundation, The Donnell-Kay Foundation, and the Sturm Family Foundation. At one point, both Gonring and Board of Education president Elaine Berman pursued funding from the Los Angeles–based Broad Foundation, which appeared to be interested. The interest, however, dissipated when the Board of Education and Superintendent Chip Zullinger came to a mutual separation agreement. Broad Foundation staff did suggest, however, that the philanthropy would continue the conversation once leadership within the district stabilized.

Denver has a relatively small foundation community, which grows smaller when sorting out the foundations willing to make grants to public education. With little "old money" to target for the remaining $3 million, Gonring knew that he would need to find a national partner with some deep pockets to keep the project moving. That both MacArthur and Broad had initially declined was a matter of grave concern. As fiscal agent of the project, Rose had bills to pay. At one point, a last-minute grant from the Denver branch of the Jay and Rose Phillips Family Foundation allowed Rose to guarantee contracts with the providers for an additional year. Although it had not anticipated having to do so when it made its first $1 million grant, Rose made another $1 million investment in the summer of 2001, still believing that changing the way teachers are paid was an idea whose time had come and that venture philanthropy was needed to make it happen. A big boost came when the Denver-based Daniels Fund, a newly formed billion-dollar foundation, came forward with a $500,000 grant, a serious contribution that provided greater legitimacy to a project that was being seen increasingly as a one-foundation show.

Early 2002 brought arguably one of the most important grants to date, a $1 million contribution from the Broad Foundation. Leadership had been stabilized with the appointment of Jerry Wartgow as superintendent, so the Broad Foundation considered DPS a good investment—the foundation was actually sponsoring a strategic support team for Wartgow. Broad program officer Veronica Davey and Becca Bracy had conducted two site visits to Denver and were impressed by the partnership among local philanthropy, DPS, and DCTA. Davey recalls the Broad Foundation's decision to make the grant after her last site visit, "Denver's pay for performance project was in a sweet spot for the Broad Foundation—our mission being to improve urban education through better management, governance and labor relations. We were enthusiastic about investing in a project led by the union that had the potential to revolutionize a management lever, teacher pay, and quality."[3]

The project now had its national partner, an organization that would prove to be an irreplaceable ProComp team member because it was willing to invest large sums of money, employ dollars flexibly, and engage as a thoughtful partner for the remainder of the effort. While PFP may have been operating behind the scenes within the school district and the union, and while it might not have gotten the help it needed from central administration, the pilot had now captured the attention of one of America's most important education philanthropies, and it now had all the funding it needed.

Back in the Skunk Works

But the pilot was still favored by few within the school district, as the effort continued to suffer from what some would call neglect. Once he became superintendent, however, Wartgow cast the pilot project in an entirely different light. He argued to Jupp that the PFP pilot should exist as a skunk works, a research and development effort operating outside normal management constraints and oversight. While Jupp failed to warm up to it immediately, the notion quickly became more attractive as Wartgow compared Jupp and the design team's work to Saturn's existence inside General Motors. The skunk works, he suggested, would free up progressive people to think creatively without being burdened by the daily politics and machinations of an urban school district.

While he may have appreciated greater responsiveness from certain sectors of the school district, Jupp realized that he and his colleagues had in fact developed a very effective skunk works. Disconnected from other major projects soon after the board and union extended the pilot, the design team was able to address flaws in the initial collective-bargaining agreement without much oversight from anyone. In fact, Gonring used to ask Jupp, "Who the hell is supervising you, anyway?" No one really knew.

As we discussed in chapter 1, a major problem with 1999's union contract was that it called for piloting three separate approaches to teacher pay, one of which was so complex it was virtually unfathomable. While until 2001 pilot schools were labeled as "approach one, two, or three" schools, for all practical purposes the three approaches had eroded quickly into one: a student growth objective-setting process. Within the skunk works, then, the design team saw that it had two purposes: first, to develop and implement the objective-setting process in the 16 pilot schools and, second, to build district capacity to support a pay system that incorporated the process. The first of these purposes was largely within the team's control. It developed procedures for principals and teachers to follow and tools, like examples of strong objectives and guidelines on how to use assessments, to measure whether objectives had been met. With CTAC, the design team developed a five-pronged objective-setting process that included not only student achievement goals based on growth but also strategies teachers would use to produce the expected gains. CTAC also helped develop rubrics to evaluate the objectives set by teachers. Members of the design team visited schools, supporting teachers and principals as they collaborated on objectives, and kept track of the rate at which objectives were developed, prodding principals if they were late in submitting them. If needed, they mediated disputes between principals and teachers. They even assisted teachers in the development of assessments while at the same time pushing unsuccessfully for central administration to develop additional methods to support teachers and principals in the objective setting process.

Building district capacity to support a new pay system was another story; it demanded work outside the design team's control. While administrators were preoccupied with other, more immediate concerns, the team did in fact experience some success. It worked with the Department of Assessment and Testing to develop two web-based systems, one that gave teachers access to student assessment histories and one for teachers to record their objectives. Both of these were hits in schools; indeed, in fall 2001, Wartgow directed that the two systems be made available to all schools, not just those engaged in the pilot.

At the same time, the design team worked with union leadership to expand its understanding of the pilot, experimenting with countless tactics, none of which worked comfortably: monthly updates to DCTA's board of directors, lunches with the executive director and committee leaders, briefings to state leaders and at TURN meetings. In all cases, team members felt welcome but like they were bringing troubling, though simple news from the teacher-compensation front: "Be careful, this just might work."

Not surprisingly, there was some friction between the design team and CTAC, the technical assistance provider and evaluator. Slotnik found that union president Becky Wissink took a very evenhanded and methodical approach to moving forward with PFP, while Jupp was more passionate, sometimes fiery. In fact, Slotnik notes that on contentious issues CTAC staff reported that dealing with Jupp could be like "swallowing razorblades."

While Jupp and his colleagues were hard at work, Wartgow orchestrated arguably one of the most important maneuvers of the pilot. In the first months of his term as superintendent, he responded to the Board of Education's demand that he prioritize the pilot among other initiatives by making two key hires from outside the system, Andre Pettigrew and Rich Allen. Pettigrew, the new assistant superintendent for operations (now DPS chief operating officer) had worked not only in private industry but also for the state of Colorado; in that capacity he had helped implement a version of PFP in state government. Allen, appointed as assistant superintendent of budget and finance, had worked for Wartgow in the state community-college system. Before hiring them, Wartgow explained that PFP would be the priority in his administration, and that if they came to work for him they would have to help him make it work.

"They came, and they were committed," Wartgow remembers, knowing that he had produced two strong supporters of PFP for his cabinet. In fact, both Allen and Pettigrew would become soldiers in the ProComp army and run interference in their departments for the design team as necessary.

But Wartgow did something else that had symbolic importance. On the organizational flow chart he prepared for the press and community, he showed Jupp as a direct report to the superintendent, a fact that certainly was not lost on many of his colleagues within the union and that may have contributed to his eventual demise as DCTA's chief negotiator. Nevertheless, Jupp actually was going to be supervised—at least symbolically! Wartgow also was skilled at public pronouncements for multiple internal and external audiences about the importance of PFP; as Slotnik remembers, the superintendent would often say, "If you didn't have PFP already put into motion in DPS, I would have had to invent it."

Actually, Jupp and his colleagues still struggled to get what they needed from portions of central administration, especially as the district rolled out its huge literacy initiative and some administrators in curriculum and instruction remained passive in their commitment to PFP. Gonring would continue to ask why representatives from instruction rarely showed up at leadership meetings, and he would be reminded that the district was overextended and was a devoting a huge amount of resources to an effort that likely would result in nothing.

The Skunk Works Expands

Late in 2001, the design team helped their skunk works spin off a new subsidiary, the JTF, a team of five teachers, five administrators, and two community members charged to design the compensation system on which the board and union would ultimately vote. The school district and union appointed as cochairs Allen and labor hero Gary Justus—a brilliant appointment because he had just won a lawsuit against the school district and by no stretch of the imagination could be accused of being in the school district's pocket.

The JTF struggled at first, as the district tried to tackle the design of the system too early and angered some members, especially teachers who believed they did not have enough information to make any decisions about how teachers should be paid. As a result, Jupp, who staffed the committee, proposed a yearlong seminar phase, which would begin in February of 2002 and produce knowledge that the JTF would use to design the new system. Here, again, the theory of learning was coming into play.

To design a compensation curriculum for that seminar phase, Jupp worked with Eric Hirsch, then the executive director of the Denver-based Alliance for Quality Teaching, a nonprofit created by Rose to help improve teacher quality in the Denver metro area. Under Hirsch's direction, the JTF first studied traditional compensation plans before moving to an examination of alternative systems, like the ones that had been tried in Minneapolis, Minnesota; Cincinnati, Ohio; Fairfax County, Virginia; and Douglas County, Colorado. They examined private pay systems, as presented by the Denver-based Mountain States Employers' Council, and studied broader issues of school finance in Colorado.

The JTF also learned from the experiences of the pilot itself. In December 2001, CTAC had presented publicly its midpoint research on PFP effort, called *Pathway to Results: Pay for Performance in Denver.* CTAC found that the early student growth objectives set by teachers in the pilot varied widely; for example, according to Slotnik, one teacher earned additional compensation for learning to use PowerPoint presentation systems. However, the study also revealed that quality objective setting was possible and that teachers in the pilot were not engaged in negative or detrimental competition with each other. CTAC also emphasized the need for utilizing consistent measures of student performance, as opposed to employing a haphazard array of teacher-developed assessments.

After reviewing the CTAC midterm study and the JTF's own analysis of efforts in the private and public sectors into the committee's theory of learning, the JTF concluded its seminar phase in February 2003, preparing to move onto the design phase for DPS's new compensation system. The task force spent the next two months debating the inclusion of the specific elements that would eventually become ProComp. Key decisions included which specific components to incorporate in the system, how to integrate these into a sustainable and not overly complex plan, and how to raise new funds to pay for the plan over time. Although CTAC would not unveil its final findings about the pilot program until January 2004, to inform the JTF's debate, Slotnik continuously fed it pertinent information from the pilot study. Allen unveiled his ingenious scheme to pursue a $25 million property-tax mill levy to fund the new system, aiming to inject new money into the system, and making what would become ProComp more palatable to the teachers who would have to vote for it.

Jupp believes that one of the most significant moments in the JTF's work was in its seeing the possibility that individual teacher impact on student learning was more important than collective teacher effects. In 1999, school-based incentives were all the rage. But in 2000 the design team had an experience in which teachers reacted negatively to a collective incentive. At the same time, all other teachers in the pilot, then nearly 350 of them, were enthusiastic about their individual incentives. The experience reinforced a conclusion first ProComp leaders and then the task force would draw again and again: teachers would rather control their own compensation destiny than leave it up to their colleagues. As a result, the JTF crafted a system that has only one small group component.

Still, however, a major bone of contention became whether the system should include a part that tied teacher pay to the state assessment. Denver teacher Jeff Buck remembers, "The obvious flashpoint was CSAP. I was probably the most vocal opponent of basing pay on CSAP scores."[4] In the end, the teachers on the committee were persuaded otherwise by Allen, who convinced the group that Denver voters would never vote to fund a plan that failed in some way to incorporate the test that had become the cornerstone of state accountability systems. Allen, according to Buck, played a crucial role during the design phase. "I learned a lot from Rich about how money works over time and how to budget responsibly," Buck admits. "Rich pushed back on my naive ideas about budgeting."

Buck's remarks show clearly the culture that developed during the seminar phase, a culture that contrasts dramatically with the picture we have of typical negotiations—with labor and management leaning over tables to throttle each other. Buck was in fact learning from Allen. Moreover, Jupp enabled the JTF to develop the system on their own, not have them react to one that came out of his own head. Buck remembers that on the task force, Jupp "wasn't really a direct participant. He functioned more as a facilitator. To a large extent he let the conversation take its course. I don't honestly think that he had a super clear vision. Being able to let it go its own way made it a stronger product. It turned out to be much more organic."

Overall, the process produced some good compromises, according to Buck: "We were able to navigate a middle way that met the needs of both parties." By the end of April 2003, therefore, the committee had produced its first draft of the new system, incorporating the four elements we described in chapter 1. The committee then sought feedback from teachers and administrators and continued to meet to discuss and make revisions based on the feedback it was getting.

One major change came from an unlikely source. The JTF had originally proposed that only teachers considered "distinguished" be eligible for the market incentives. One would think that the union might oppose such a distinction; however, central administration, in fact, argued it did not have the tools to decide who was "distinguished" and who was not. As a result, ProComp now offers small incentives to teachers who are rated as satisfactory and does not give much larger rewards to teachers rated as above that standard.

By the end of 2003, after several months of review and discussion, the JTF called it a day. The committee had devised and labeled a salary system that was ready to go to teachers for their approval or rejection. The system, which would come to be called ProComp, had—depending on one's vantage point—either survived or thrived within Wartgow's skunk works.

Marginalized but Successful

Union reform leader Adam Urbanski likes to remind audiences of the business school truism that "if you have more than one first priority, you in fact have no priorities at all." There were certainly too many top priorities in DPS from February 2000 to December 2003. We will leave it to others to explore whether this flaw is endemic to large public-sector organizations like school districts. In hindsight, however, we can say that Denver's PFP pilot, as well as its significant spin-off, the JTF, thrived in this environment. Its leaders took advantage of almost all the tools at their disposal—from halfhearted support to total neglect—and used them to sculpt and unveil a substantially different model of teacher pay. The breakthroughs of this period—especially the abandonment of a salary schedule used to pigeonhole teachers into a limited number of steps and the need to procure additional tax dollars to pay for the new compensation system—were unlikely to have been made in the course of debate among status quo policy leaders. In this sense, the long period of neglect proved the best thing that happened to Denver's PFP pilot. In the end, Wartgow gave the members of the design team and the JTF the free space they needed to think independently from organizational constraints and develop ProComp, a system that was the product of either genius or dumb luck or perhaps a combination of both.

4

Winning Votes and Influencing People

"Our Members Would Have Killed Us"

n the hierarchy of school parties, potluck is king. As a result, one must never underestimate the power of throwing a real party for teachers, of treating them like the people seen wearing tuxedoes and gowns in the society sections of big-city newspapers, of serving them cheese and fancy hors d'oeuvres and letting them know that their work really matters, especially when they are trying to do things differently and their colleagues are yelling at them. They may actually come to believe their work is every bit as important to the community as the opening of a brand-new concert hall or library—and so will the broader community if the shindig is covered by the press.

Over the life of the PFP pilot, several of the Denver-based philanthropies threw lots of parties, as both a tactic and an ethical act. The foundations were of course counting votes, thinking that happy teachers in pilot schools would become hard-working advocates for ProComp. But they also wanted to give hardworking, risk-taking teachers and administrators their due. So they annually hosted breakfasts and lunches at each of the pilot schools. Over eggs benedict or steak and fancy potatoes, members of the board of education and the PFP design team, foundation executives, and board members thanked the teachers for their groundbreaking efforts in piloting PFP.

At one school, a principal cried, tearfully remarking that no one had ever treated her teachers so kindly. At another, teachers announced how they would be spending their bonus checks, with one third-grade teacher shouting out that she was going to purchase a stove she had had her eye on for the last three years.

At key junctures of the pilot, the foundations also hosted even more elegant receptions, designed to signal the import of an event or rally the faithful to an important cause. To mark the end of the second year of the pilot and the release of CTAC's midterm report, for instance, school board member Les Woodward arranged for a reception at Denver's posh University Club, where it is likely that not many Denver teachers are members.

And, so it was in January 2004 that the foundations arranged perhaps the most important event to date, the public presentation of CTAC's final report coupled with a reception to honor those who had made the pilot possible. In the large conference room of a Denver hotel, union leaders, school board members, school district employees, pilot-school teachers, foundation executives, and the press gathered to listen to Bill Slotnik and his team present their research. Slotnik focused the audience on key findings, which are enumerated in CTAC's final report, *Catalyst for Change: Pay for Performance in Denver*.[1]

The report is remarkably thorough and comprehensive—CTAC conducted more than 600 interviews with participants and other parties, reviewed over 4,000 teacher objectives and created a database to link teachers and students in the 16 pilot and control schools, among many other tasks, to produce the study. CTAC's far-reaching report reminds its readers that changing teacher pay is about more than reorganizing the way money is given out; it requires school districts to rethink how they function: "The pilot has been a catalyst for changing the district so that it could become focused on student achievement in a more coordinated and consolidated way." The report continues, "The changes required to identify, strengthen and reward individual student growth and individual teacher contributions under pay for performance have the added effect of stimulating other parts of the school system to improve the quality of support and service."[2]

For future teacher-compensation reformers, this point is key, and the magnitude of the change to which Slotnik and his coauthors are referring will be the subject of chapter 6, in which we detail the profound systems-change work that Brad Jupp and others would oversee. While the point about systemic change in support of compensation reform is significant, we turn our attention to the finding that at the time trumped all others.

The cornerstone of the PFP pilot was the student growth objective-setting process. As part of its research design, CTAC developed a rubric to evaluate the quality of the objectives that every teacher in the pilot worked with her principal to create. As Slotnik announced that night, the quality of student growth objectives had an impact on student learning over the life of the pilot. The impact is noted in the CTAC report:

> At all three academic levels—elementary, middle, and high school—higher mean student achievement in the pilot schools is positively associated with the highest quality objectives. Students whose teachers had excellent objectives, based on a four-level rubric developed by CTAC, achieved higher mean scores than students whose teachers' objectives were scored lower in the rubric. This holds true on most tests of the Iowa Test of Basic Skills (ITBS) and the Colorado Student Assessment Program (CSAP).[3]

This finding was critical for the future of ProComp. Of its impact on the union's ability to move forward with the development of the new compensation system, DCTA's executive director, Bruce Dickinson, remarks, "We could not have gone forward without having that kind of backup. We just couldn't have. Our members would have killed us."[4] It satisfied the most difficult aspect of the criteria DCTA president Becky Wissink had established for the pilot and any future compensation system: Does it have a positive impact on student achievement? Indeed, as the CTAC report suggested, it did. The road home had now been paved by CTAC's findings. Within the span of a few weeks, the JTF would have to travel that road to deliver to the Board of Education and DCTA not only a finalized compensation system but also the negotiated agreement governing its implementation.

Winter Break and Beyond

Fortunately, Jupp had some time off. Between December 27 and January 4, he wrote the first draft of the agreement governing ProComp, one the union and the board would have to ratify if the new compensation system was to become a reality. Gleaning from his notes on nearly two years of JTF conversations, Jupp "beat it into contract language," remembers task-force member Jeff Buck.[5]

Through 72 hours of meetings that spanned the month of January, the group worked line by line through Jupp's draft, editing with great care, making significant changes and producing what Jupp calls "a far better document" than the one he wrote on vacation. With appendixes, the document is quite long, covering minute details such as integrating Junior ROTC teachers in ProComp, but it mainly focuses on much broader policy details, not the least of which is the four-component framework for ProComp: knowledge and skills, professional evaluation, market incentives, and student growth, which we enumerated in chapter 1.

Yet the document is remarkable for its other accomplishments. It establishes a transition team made up of five teachers and five administrators who will "monitor the phase-in of the professional compensation system" and "develop, implement and evaluate the transition plan," identifying work that must be done to successfully implement ProComp.[6] Moreover, it prevents the school district from establishing quotas, meaning that neither the board of education nor a heavy-handed superintendent can ever say only a certain number of teachers are eligible for knowledge and skills pay, for example.

Some aspects of the agreement merit more detailed discussion, particularly three of its major accomplishments. First, it creates a financial lockbox for all dollars generated to support the new system. Next, it institutionalizes the primacy of ongoing learning by requiring continuous evaluation that can be used by the union and district in negotiations to actually make adjustments to the compensation system. Finally, to the delight of organizations out to minimize the amount of litigation in public life, it sends lawyers packing, placing dispute resolution in the hands of teachers and administrators.

As members of the JTF completed the agreement, it imagined the two elections that faced them, the union vote to ratify ProComp and the public election to generate the $25 million required to support the new system. The need for a trust fund, one of the avant-garde requirements of the agreement, is obvious in light of labor management politics. "Would future boards of education pillage mill-levy funds to pay for textbooks or administrative salaries during hard financial times?" a reasonable teacher might ask. This question is fair and relevant, for during the 2004 school year, arts-education advocates accused DPS of failing to spend dollars generated by 2003's successful mill levy on art teachers, as promised in the campaign and by the ballot language citizens of Denver had approved. The ProComp framers sought to alleviate any lingering doubts in the public's and teaching corps's minds by taking spending authority away from the board of education and giving it to the Board of Directors of the ProComp Trust Fund:

> The Board of Directors . . . has the fiduciary responsibility to ensure that funds of trust shall be spent only on the Professional Compensation System for Teachers and only in keeping with the terms and conditions of this Agreement, the ballot language approved by the voters in the mill levy override election and the goals of the Professional Compensation System for Teachers. Should the Board of Directors at any time determine that the funds have not been spent on the Professional Compensation System for Teachers, or according to the terms and conditions of this Agreement and the goals of the Professional Compensation System for Teachers, or in a manner in keeping with the ballot language approved by the voters in the mill levy override election, then the Board has the duty to stop transmitting the funds of the Trust to the District.[7]

A board populated only by administrators, a teacher might argue, would never vote to stop transmitting funds to the school district, so the framers of the agreement gave the union president the power to appoint three representatives. They would be joined by the treasurer of the Board of Education, the school district's chief financial officer, and the assistant superintendent for budget and finance. These six members would in turn appoint two community representatives. Besides receiving mill-levy dollars and monitoring their expenditure by the school district, the Board of Directors is required to develop and maintain a long-term financial model for the system, invest fund balances, and annually commission an external audit of the trust's revenues and expenditures. First, however, the board's job would be to ensure that teachers, and no one else, got the money.

While the trust fund imagined future elections and created a lockbox for voter-approved ProComp tax dollars, other requirements of the ProComp Agreement institutionalized the theory of learning begun in the pilot by allowing elements of the compensation system to "be adjusted through the collective bargaining process based on experience and the financial model." The agreement requires the district and union to jointly commission an annual internal evaluation as well as a longer-term third party evaluation. The internal evaluation will include an "analysis of the implementation of the system and its effectiveness at achieving District and Association mission and goals."[8]

Based on the analysis, the transition team will annually develop recommendations for improvement. For instance, the team may determine that professional-development services principals receive about the objective-setting process need to be modified or that the PDUs need refinement.

Slated to be presented by November 2009, the third-party evaluation established by the agreement is designed to examine multiple years of data and offer findings and recommendation for improvement of the system to support 2009's negotiations around ProComp. If, for example, the researchers conclude that the market incentives for hard-to-staff schools are not large enough, then the union and school district might in their 2009 negotiations consider increasing the amount of money paid to teachers working in tough schools and decreasing the incentives paid teachers who reach other milestones. A similar negotiation is imagined for December 31, 2013, when the initial agreement expires and another will need to be negotiated, likely becoming a component of the master DPS-union contract and ceasing its existence as a stand-alone document.

Finally, putting dispute resolution into the hands of principals' and teachers' peers, the agreement actually strips attorneys of the roles they normally play in resolving conflict. If, for instance, a teacher disagrees with a compensation decision related to ProComp, the "decision shall be reviewed by a teacher and an administrator or principal randomly selected from the Professional Review Panel," a body of five DCTA members and five principals and administrators selected through an interview process administered by the transition team.[9] The aggrieved teacher presents her case to the panel at a hearing in which the "decision-making administrator" also gets to make her case. The agreement encourages those hearing the dispute to reach consensus; however, if they cannot, the original compensation decision is final. When a decision is final, it is also binding, putting attorneys, judges, and arbitrators out of the business of administering ProComp.

The JTF itself would soon be out of business as well, as January 2004 neared its end and its members put the finishing touches on Pro-Comp's constitution. The task force's work would soon be read in faculty lounges and school offices throughout the city, the basis for a vote by Denver's teachers. As they took time to leaf through the agreement, let us hope that regardless of their opinion of ProComp, they found the work remarkable, worthy of hanging in the National Education Association's Washington offices—not from a rope, but on a wall, gilded and framed. While Jupp cannot weigh in without bias, Phil Gonring and Paul Teske believe the agreement exemplary, an illustration of what can be accomplished if an urban school district's bureaucrats and teachers have the time and resources to think, analyze, and develop policy. The ProComp Agreement is a tribute to the genius within the union and DPS.

Buck suggests that the agreement stands as proof that "cooperation can get you further than confrontational behavior." He additionally explains the process that led to the production of the document: "It was a negotiation in a way that was a positive thing. Labor negotiation is unproductive in my opinion. This was not like that. It was often contentious, but we were able to solve contention in a respectful way." It was soon to become clear, however, that though it may have been a work of genius, ProComp appeared headed for the gallows, as the result of a great deal of contention.

A Near-Death Experience

Everywhere one looked, the news was bad. ProComp supporters publicly suggested that the union did not have to approve ProComp for the pilot to be a success; Gonring made the claim to Rose's Education Committee, repeating what he had heard over and over again from representatives of DPS and other foundations. Even the final CTAC report suggested that all would not be lost if the ship went down at sea: "Regardless of whether a new compensation plan passes or not, Pay for Performance will have an impact."[10]

Gonring had taken to surveying teachers informally wherever he encountered them—in schools, at parties, in the grocery store. As the JTF completed its work, he met a former colleague in the produce section of his neighborhood supermarket. A decade earlier, the woman was a newly-minted teacher, fresh out of college. She loved teaching English; smart and passionate about her work, she was exactly the kind of teacher we want working in urban education. Gonring remembers the interaction clearly.

"ProComp is horrible," the teacher pronounced with a great deal of authority. "What don't you like about it?" Gonring asked, trying to sound detached and scientific.

"I don't know," she said less assuredly. "But the union representative in my building thinks it stinks so I'm voting against it."

She went on to report that her opinion did not really matter anyway because she was tired of working in a district that paid her far less money than others would. In fact, she had recently accepted a job in one of Denver's more affluent suburbs, where she knew she would not have to work as hard but make $8,000 a year more than DPS had been paying her. Not persuaded by the suggestion that a talented teacher like her could make a lot more money under ProComp, she said she was too frustrated by DPS to stay anyway.

Time after time, teachers complained, "ProComp is unfair," or, "I teach in a low-income school, so it will be much harder for me to get a raise," or "My master's degree will become useless"—inaccuracies all. With misinformation spilling out in anecdotes in large enough quantities, Rose's Education Committee and Gonring began to doubt the efficacy of the $160,000 grant it had given to the union to communicate with its members about ProComp. He and Veronica Davey of the Broad Foundation also worried that while the communication materials they had funded had been some of the best they had ever seen and were very effective for audiences external to the school district, they may have been too detailed for internal audiences. Teachers, as school urban legend suggests, need things they can read between their mailboxes and the "circular file," the trash can in the hallway.

Gonring had begun to believe that if ProComp was going to be approved by teachers, someone was going to have to mount a campaign within the union. For more than four years, Jupp already had been suggesting that the union eventually would need to organize in schools as if it were preparing for a strike. He envisioned a "war room" within the union hall, dividing the district into quadrants, with teams of organizers fanning across the city, holding faculty meetings, identifying concerns and questions and then visiting the schools a second and a third time, conducting one-on-one meetings with teachers and establishing a call center so that teachers could have their questions answered any time during the day. But this was not likely to happen, Jupp thought, because the union did not know how to switch from a posture of neutrality to one of advocacy. In fact, when Wissink went into buildings to talk about ProComp, she told teachers she was neutral; it was the members who would get to make the decision about ProComp. "I get to break the tie if there is one," she recalls telling her members.[11]

Recall that the union had to remain neutral about pay for performance for over five years, as the pilot played out and as the CTAC report was produced. Engineering a shift to a position of advocacy from one of neutrality was undoubtedly made more difficult because the neutral role had become routine. Yet it had become clear to the philanthropies that their investment was at risk, that millions of taxpayer dollars potentially had been misspent on a pipe dream, that the Denver community was likely to miss out on a tremendous opportunity to rethink teacher pay, and that the national dialogue around teacher compensation would be set back yet again.

At this point, however, the philanthropies had only anecdotal data and union reports to support their opinion that ProComp was about to be added to the dustbin of educational reform. To get a better grip on the gravity of the situation and potentially bolster the case for a campaign, Rose commissioned Paul Talmey, a well-regarded political pollster, to survey Denver teachers about ProComp, to find out how the election was likely to unfold and what, if anything, could be done to produce a favorable result.

If anyone had still been hopeful that ProComp would pass, the results of Talmey's poll dashed those hopes quickly: 19 percent of DCTA members indicated they would vote to approve, 59 percent to oppose— with 21 percent undecided. Moreover, only 8 percent of those undecided were leaning toward an affirmative vote. Talmey also offered advice for a potential campaign, suggesting that teachers should be shown they could make considerably more money in the new system and that no one would make less. He also reminded ProComp supporters that the "campaign must also overcome deep concerns about how the new system will be administered, and a general distrust of DPS's administration to implement it fairly. The campaign will need to show that most of the criteria for salary increases and bonuses are objective and not at the whim of the administration."[12] Talmey's summary concludes ominously, however:

> All that said, it's hard to be optimistic about the outcome of this election. Too many teachers seem distrustful not only of the administration, but of change itself. The current compensation system based on seniority plus academic training is very secure, and those who have been in the system for more than a few years are very reluctant to see it go away. Teachers with 14 or more years of DPS service are more distrustful of the administration with 69 percent strongly agreeing with the statement: "The proposed new system will put too much power

over how much teachers are compensated in the hands of administrators . . . ," a much higher percentage than among those with fewer years of service. Moreover, an incredible 74 percent of teachers who have 14 years or more service with DPS say they will vote against the proposed compensation system. One cannot help but suspect that these teachers see little gain for themselves from implementing the new system, while feeling that in some unknown way that it threatens their security—if only in the potential for younger and newer teachers to financially outperform them.[13]

Neither the anecdotal evidence nor the data looked very good. After five years of work and the expenditure of millions of dollars, why did the project appear headed for the gallows? Gonring's encounter with the teacher in the supermarket and the data produced by Talmey suggest multiple answers and make clear the magnitude of the challenge ProComp advocates faced.

Gonring remains steadfast in his belief that over the life of the pilot the union and the philanthropies should have engaged the union's building representatives much more thoughtfully so that they felt involved and had a stake in the development of ProComp. Perhaps, then, some would not have spread misinformation or venom about ProComp in their schools. Further, in retrospect, the communication efforts coming out of the design team and funded by the philanthropies had not accomplished what face-to-face meetings likely would have.

As the data and anecdotes suggest, however, there were many more factors than skeptical building representatives and communications problems that accounted for the poor support teachers showed for ProComp five weeks before the election. For instance, it could be argued that any communication effort would have been destined to fail. Wissink reminds us that teachers in only 16 schools actually piloted PFP. Within those schools, only 263 teachers participated from beginning to end, while over 1,000 taught in pilot schools between 1999 and 2003. Two of the 12 elementary school principals oversaw ProComp pilot schools from beginning to end of the PFP effort, and the vast majority of district principals knew little about the pilot other than that while it might mean more pay for teachers, it meant only more work for no more pay for those in administration. In fact, Wissink remembers that some principals told teachers ProComp was "a bad deal." Having four superintendents between the time the union agreed to pilot PFP and March 2004 no doubt further complicated communication efforts and made it more difficult to nurture trust between labor and management.

This absence of trust was probably exacerbated by the fact that not all the procedural details of ProComp had been finalized. If a teacher did not trust her employer, she might wonder how "hard-to-staff" and "distinguished" schools would be defined and what the new professional evaluation toolkit would look like. Moreover, as the Talmey poll suggests, many teachers wondered if DPS would have the capacity to administer such a complicated system; some are still wondering this more than two years after the union election. Jupp, however, believes it would have been foolish and impossible to develop fully all of the procedures prior to the vote and that ProComp, as policy, was as thoroughly developed as many other initiatives teachers had encountered as citizens when they voted on ballot initiatives in general elections. Jupp thinks that most teachers who raised the issue of the absence of procedural details were using that as an excuse to vote "no."

Finally, as the teacher in the supermarket reminds us, money was an issue affecting teacher support for ProComp. We cannot underestimate the extreme financial difficulties confronting DPS as it undertook the pilot and prepared for permanent implementation. When Jerry Wartgow took office, over $17 million in recurring operating expenses were annually being paid using onetime money. The district's stand alone pension system, isolated from the state's Public Employee Retirement Association (PERA), cost the district twice the employer contribution that it would have were it a PERA partner. Further, under pressure from the state and community, DPS has become remarkably charter-school friendly. At least in the short run, growing charter-school enrollments have an adverse effect on school-district budgets that are difficult to remediate with highly contentious school closures or consolidations. As enrollment has declined in DPS, it has become overbuilt, with far too many dollars going to support underutilized facilities.

These financial burdens, coupled with a lack of ingenuity at the bargaining table, made it difficult to avoid acrimonious contract negotiations. In 2003 the union reluctantly accepted a wage freeze, as the district believed it could not offer a cost-of-living increase or the traditional steps for experience on the salary schedule. In return for this concession, the district cut three teacher workdays. The union made a brief and unsuccessful bid to recoup these lost wages by arguing that teacher salaries should be added to that year's mill-levy campaign, an effort designed to raise funds to pay for art teachers and special school-innovation grants. Rebuffed, the union did not endorse the mill levy, further fueling animosity between the superintendent's office and the union, which continued to argue that it needed to recoup the wages lost in the settlement.

ProComp advocates hoped that by the time teachers voted on the new salary system, the district and union would have settled harmoniously. Despite efforts of some within the union to couple the 2004 settlement with the ProComp agreement—even going so far to argue that teachers should not vote on ProComp until the contract was settled, this linkage did not occur. Still, the JTF-created agreement headed for a vote with teacher anger simmering about the lost step, resentment that no doubt contributed to Gonring's former colleague, the one he'd met in the supermarket, leaving the school district and to a discontented membership ready to vote ProComp down by an overwhelming margin.

A Fateful Decision

Davey remembers the results Gonring communicated to her as generating concern but ultimately readying her to roll up her sleeves and get to work. The philanthropies, after all, had gotten used to having obstacles thrown in the path of the pilot and now the vote. Gonring and Davey began thinking about how they would have to couple the bad news with a solution. In fact, Rose's education committee had for some time been talking about paying for a campaign to win the vote, which they would have preferred to avoid. With Talmey's data in front of them, Gonring and Davey spoke even more intensely about pushing for a political campaign. In the absence of a union-led campaign like the one Jupp conceived, they would consider promoting an effort outside the auspices of the union—although hopefully with union leadership's blessing. They consulted Jupp, but at this point they were not asking for his permission and would likely have moved forward without his support.

Jupp recollects that he knew Gonring and Davey were feeling nervous even though he reminded them that strike votes often come from far behind as well and that traditional poll interpretation might not work for a situation like the ProComp election. But he also suggests that they primarily understood the magnitude of the moment. If Denver teachers voted to adopt it, ProComp was going to transform the teacher-salary policy debate on both local and national levels, probably permanently. Among the two program officers, there was talk that if the foundations were not able to take advantage of the current project, there might never come an opportunity again, and the Denver venture would stand as final proof that teacher unions would never accept a real alternative to the single salary schedule. They feared that failure would set compensation reform back for years.

As luck would have it, the day after Talmey released the results of the survey, Gonring met with school board member Elaine Berman at a lunch meeting at the Wynkoop Brewery, where he detailed for her the sobering results of the survey and thought aloud about how they might get a campaign effort started. As her penchant is to grasp for solutions, Berman immediately thought of John Britz, partner in the political consulting firm Welchert and Britz, an organization she knew had a long history of working with teacher unions. Having served with his partner as the Colorado state teachers association's general political consultant and grown up in a household in which teacher-union politics was the subject of dinner-table conversation—Britz's dad has been a longtime teacher-union employee—Britz and his colleague Steve Welchert were uniquely positioned to help change the course of the election.

Although recollections differ, it is likely that a meeting was held the very next day on the seventh floor of the DPS administrative offices. Wissink, for the union; Berman and Woodward, from the Board of Education; Superintendent Wartgow and some of his key staff; Gonring, from Rose; and Britz discussed the poll results and the possibility of mounting a campaign. Gonring called the question: To get ProComp passed, would everyone support a Britz-led effort in consultation with the union?

Those involved in the meeting do not have the same opinion as to whether the parties were being asked to agree to an informational campaign or an all-out effort to win the election. Regardless, everyone agreed to move forward, understanding that the campaign would meet regularly with union leaders and coordinate tactics with them, although there is also some debate about whether the coordination actually happened in a way that was satisfactory to all parties.

What Rose wanted was made clear to the consultants in their contract: their job was to win. This was probably a unique moment in philanthropy, as a community foundation decided that by intervening in a teacher-union election it would be advancing a charitable cause: improving the quality of teaching for Denver's children.

As often happens in philanthropy, foundation officers, in this case Davey and Gonring, had to couch their commitment to fund the campaign in tentative terms. They each had to seek the approval of either a board committee or donor. It would be a mistake to underestimate the willingness of the decisionmakers at the foundations to be flexible, to make decisions quickly, and to provide funding that was not limited to any construct they had imposed when they first made their grants. The 19 percent to 58 percent voter gap was not a construct they had imagined when they first engaged the project.

On February 17, just five days after Talmey released his polling results, Rose's education committee met to discuss the survey data and to consider funding the Welchert-Britz effort. By now well acquainted with the ebb and flow of the project, committee members did not despair at Talmey's polling results. Failure was not an option, and the committee was going to keep working, believing that once teachers really learned about the system, they would approve it. Committee chair Lydia Peña remembers lines from an Emily Dickinson poem that capture the committee's spirit: "Hope is the thing with feathers / that perches in the soul, / and sings the tune without the words, /and never stops at all."[14] Rose's president Sheila Bugdanowitz recalled Denver Bronco and Hall of Famer John Elway's famous quote before orchestrating "The Drive" in the 1986 NFL season's AFC divisional championship game. Finding his team 98 yards from a touchdown with only a few minutes remaining in the game, Elway famously remarked, "We've got them right where we want them."[15]

Following Peña and Bugdanowitz's lead, the committee members' reactions could not be more reflective of Don Kortz's original vision for how the foundation should take risks. They authorized a grant to fund the campaign, understanding that Rose likely would not be alone, as the Broad Foundation would decide in a matter of days to join the effort not just in spirit but with a great deal of money.

Davey recollects that although the Broad Foundation realized very early on that there was no guarantee that the pilot would result in a commitment to a districtwide PFP system, she had not anticipated that the election would become a major hurdle. Once she and Gonring had reviewed the polling data and talked about the need for a campaign, she called Eli Broad to get his reaction. Davey recalls that he encouraged her to get the job done in Denver. Taking his encouragement as "a green light to move forward fast and without the usual tight knit processes," she convened an internal meeting of her colleagues to get their best thinking so she could get smarter and increase her own accountability. She later wrote a one-page memo to Broad who then authorized a significant contribution to the campaign.[16]

For Rose and for the Broad Foundation, if the teachers did not approve ProComp now, they might never. Davey recalls her excitement about the campaign. Having worked on a ballot initiative and run the campaigns of school board candidates in Los Angeles, she recollects that "it was exhilarating and challenging to have a taste of politics in the world of philanthropy." In fact, both Davey and Gonring acknowledge that while they were motivated by the desire to improve public education, with so much personal investment, they were also deeply driven by a desire to win.

Overwhelming Force

Welchert and Britz inhabit a world that is far less nurturing than those of schools and philanthropy. Callers put on hold at their offices are entertained by local sports talk-radio hosts who are, on any given day, complaining about the Broncos' quarterback, the Rockies' ownership, or the Nuggets' shooting. Both businessmen have significant athletic achievements in their past. A former offensive lineman for the University of Iowa, Welchert cuts an imposing figure at 6 foot 3 inches, looking like he could still take on the best defensive tackles in the Big 10.

"We have a competitive focus. Our detractors might suggest that makes us bullies," Welchert offers in frank assessment of how he and his partner are perceived.[17]

"We are not diplomats," the former football and state-champion lacrosse player Britz concurs. "It's almost like a locker-room mentality around here. I don't mean it's slapping people with towels and using four-letter words, but it's very competitive and there's only one outcome we want, and that's to win."[18]

Providing greater definition to the way they work, Welchert reflects that his firm brings "a Republican style to liberal politics," suggesting that he and Britz bring an aggressive approach to the political campaigns they run, including the one they managed and won in November 2006 in one of the nation's most competitive congressional districts. In addition to running state and national house and senate races, Welchert and Britz have developed strong relationships with Colorado's school districts, as well as state and local union affiliates. They run tax initiatives for a majority of the Denver metropolitan-area school districts. They have also been employed as the general political consultants for the Colorado Education Association (CEA) and often run school board races.

"We hit them over the head with a baseball bat," Britz says, describing the campaign to win the ProComp vote, a campaign that some believed would require a significant level of force, given the fact it had to be run in one month. To help level his swing, Britz had a conversation with his father, who, as someone who understands union work, concurred with Jupp's assessment of what needed to happen. Father suggested to son that he set up a "war room," divide the city into quadrants, hire organizers, and, especially, communicate one-on-one with teachers.

Welchert and Britz were clear with both Davey and Gonring, however; they did not believe they could likely turn such a serious deficit into victory, offering that the best they could probably accomplish would be to whittle away at the opposition, increase support, and perhaps set the stage for a successful future election, potentially the following year. Jupp remained more upbeat, thinking of the campaign as a boutique election and contrasting it with the state- or districtwide elections that political consultants are used to running. He believed they would have an easier time picking up the 32 points they needed in an election whose voters were held captive within schools and who had yet to get anything near full information on ProComp. Once they were informed, he thought, they would likely vote "yes."

Using financial resources provided by the philanthropies, the campaign operated a top-notch, traditional union organizing effort. They hired four super-organizers: the former president of the CEA, two former local union presidents, and a renowned grassroots political organizer. Grant funds further enabled the full-time release of four teachers whose efforts—along with those of about 20 more teachers who spent a full day or two or a few hours before and after school working on the campaign—would be coordinated by the super-organizers.

Although the attempt to label campaign headquarters as the "war room" was resisted by some within the union, Welchert and Britz established their command center, regardless of its name, in basement office space in downtown Denver. There the organizers met, charted strategy, counted votes, and fanned out to schools. On flip-chart paper, they recorded ongoing vote tallies school by school, deciding that some schools held promise, while others did not, focusing their efforts where they thought they had a chance. Although single teachers or organizers were assigned entire elementary schools, other organizers received single floors of some of the large high schools as their assignments. There, they talked to teachers before and after school, during planning periods, over lunch, in hallways, in structured or unstructured settings.

They armed themselves with campaign buttons, suggesting in hot-pink letters to teachers: "Control Your Future."

Greg Ahrnsbrak, a physical education teacher at Bruce Randolph Middle School and longtime ProComp advocate, organized in more than 10 buildings. There, he reports, he found teachers "completely uninformed," despite the notebooks full of communications they had received about the project. He and his colleagues also found numerous "closet ProCompers" in hostile territory, those teachers who planned to vote "yes" but did not want their colleagues to know their intentions, lest they suffer the wrath of those opposed to ProComp.[19] Another organizer, and Brad Jupp's wife, Chrisanne LaHue, recalls that many teachers did not verbalize support for ProComp because "the fear was so strong." While they might vote to approve ProComp in a secret ballot, they were not willing to wear one of the hot-pink buttons.[20]

Ahrnsbrak remembers, as polling data suggested, that the biggest obstacle in the buildings was the lack of trust. "Even though you can lay out a logical approach to increasing teacher pay and accountability in a fair and equitable way, you would still hear things like, 'Well, you know what the district did to me 10 years ago. Ten years ago, goddamn it, I got transferred out of my building.'" He reports that many teachers did not believe their principals were competent enough to administer ProComp, or, if they felt their current principals could, they worried that future school leaders might not have the requisite abilities. An obvious advocate of the new system, Ahrnsbrak is critical of some of his colleagues, giving his impression of the worries some had about the role of the principal: "There was so much of that typical archaic Neanderthal thinking that this couldn't be good because the principal would have control over your money."

LaHue recalls an amusing incident that demonstrated the lack of trust extended to her husband, Jupp, and that he was seen increasingly as an arm of DPS administration. Since the couple does not share a last name, many teachers do not know that Jupp and LaHue are in fact married. LaHue recounts that she was organizing in one of Denver's toughest high schools, one of the most hostile to ProComp. "I knew I was up against the hardest audience ever," she reflects, referring to a lunchtime crowd of about 10 teachers, most of whom were seasoned veterans. "I wound up debating the oldsters, knowing that I was selling the youngsters. But then they started getting personal about Brad Jupp, suggesting, 'Brad Jupp's gonna get rich off this.'" LaHue still laughs about this today, as she remembers the thousands of dollars in salary he routinely turned down in administrative job offers from the district.

Still another organizer reflects on the "culture of misinformation" that was rampant in schools. "It's a lot easier to listen to the person at lunch who says that ProComp is a bad idea than to research what it really is," Beth Douma remarks.[21] LaHue concurs, remembering the numerous times that teachers struggled to find proof to back the assertion that ProComp was not good for teachers, assertions that we have learned were sometimes promulgated by building representatives.

On top of the trust and the culture issue was the simple fact that DPS, like all large districts, employed hundreds of new teachers. Douma reflects that these teachers were simply struggling to learn their craft and did not have time to think about ProComp, let alone research the differences between it and the existing system.

Beverly Ausfahl, former president of the CEA and super-organizer on the ProComp campaign, succinctly sums up what campaign workers found: "There were people at all stages of acceptance or rejection." She believes attitudes changed and the election was eventually won because of the face-to-face meetings by both the development team and the organizers: "We found that a lot of people who had been negative began to be intrigued. The fact that people could choose to never enter the ProComp project changed minds too."[22]

Yet the campaign included much more than the efforts of organizers like Ahrnsbrak, LaHue, and Douma. It instituted a 1-800 line so that teachers could determine the differences between their salaries in the current and proposed systems. It arranged for flyers to be distributed in schools and placed in teachers' mailboxes. The campaign orchestrated a press conference with Denver's popular mayor, John Hickenlooper. On the steps of Denver's East High School, the mayor promised teachers that he would campaign for a tax increase if they voted to adopt ProComp. He also appeared in a streaming video the campaign produced and emailed to all teachers in the final days of the campaign—although it turned out to be difficult for many teachers to actually open the message.

While the campaign raged and union leadership adhered to its posture of neutrality, ProComp wound its way through normal union processes. Before the union mailed ballots to schools, its representative council would have to decide to endorse or oppose ProComp or to remain neutral. During the night of the meeting at which the teachers would vote, ProComp supporters, including Jeff Buck, implemented a floor strategy that Jupp refers to as an organized demonstration of force. Union advocates of the new system prepared teachers for debate in advance of the meeting, made sure they would present thoughtful reasons for their support, then ensured they were given time at the microphone. They came prepared to wield parliamentary procedures to extend debate as necessary and to ensure that the vote would be called for once they thought they had the votes to win. In the end, Dickinson recollects that about two-thirds voted to endorse ProComp, although this would not translate to active support outside the union hall. In internal union communications, however, the message would be sent that ProComp had the endorsement of the representative council, which teachers could weigh as they examined ballots that were now in their buildings.

With a press conference slated for the afternoon of March 20, DCTA president Wissink prepared two separate speeches, one for a ProComp victory, the other for its defeat. It was beginning to feel more and more like Wissink was going to break out the victory speech. Davey, who kept close tabs on the campaign by speaking regularly to Gonring, Welchert, and Britz and by visiting schools with organizers, reported that teachers she spoke to were actually thankful for organizations they perceived as providing neutral information. Further, visits to the war room to listen to end-of-day debriefing sessions among the organizers led Gonring and Davey to believe the tide was beginning to turn. Face-to-face meetings appeared to be paying off. In fact, midway through the 30-day campaign effort, Welchert and Britz conducted another poll of teachers, which showed that the bar had moved substantially, with 33 percent claiming they would vote to support of ProComp.

Wissink employed retired DCTA members to count the votes. She also secured the participation of the League of Women Voters to ensure the accuracy of the count. When the dust had cleared, Wissink was able to stride to the microphone with the speech announcing ProComp's passage in hand. In an election with one of the highest participation rates in DCTA history, 59 percent of the union's members had voted to support the Professional Compensation System for Teachers. Mayor Hickenlooper, Superintendent Wartgow, and board president Woodward joined Wissink in the union offices to celebrate the success. Wartgow beamed: "The eyes of educators and education policy-makers across the nation are on Denver."[23] Mayor Hickenlooper added, "I'm so excited [teachers] banded together and saw the potential."[24]

Those with their fingers in the air no doubt felt the breath exhaled by ProComp advocates, as the campaign had produced a win. ProComp was alive and well, moving ahead to a public vote that, in advocates' minds, could be nothing but positive. Never before had a major urban union successfully navigated such turbulent waters, a fact that passed through at least a couple of taverns the night after the union announced the election results. Yet ProComp supporters made merry far too soon, as more trouble lay ahead.

5

At What Cost Victory?

There Is No Next Year

ProComp had now been approved by Denver teachers, but at what cost? To some, the campaign seemed overkill, although opinions differed as to where it crossed the line from appropriate to extreme. There was also debate about whether the effort should have been informational or an outright effort to win.

Union president Becky Wissink, was clear that she had wanted the campaign to be educational. Some of her members expressed to her concern that the information in the campaign was skewed to the positive only, that it failed to present a balanced perspective and, moreover, Wissink remembers, it "came out on glossy, fancy materials, not on normal union paper."[1]

"Why didn't we have this level of information campaign for other programs and initiatives?" some of her members asked. Further, she remembers complaints that "philanthropists were trying to buy the vote with fancy materials." Union executive director Bruce Dickinson concurs with Wissink: "They don't usually get slick stuff." Additionally, the complaints came: there were people walking up and down school hallways answering questions about ProComp, and this was not the way the union typically did business. Further, school board members actually made time to campaign for ProComp when they failed to take time to visit schools for other efforts. The campaign really "raised suspicions,"

Dickinson concludes. "It was as if DCTA had lost control and the outside people had taken over."[2]

Brad Jupp, however, believes that the advocacy effort was appropriate and wishes it could have been run directly out of the union hall. He thinks, however, that the election could have been won mainly by employing the organizing tactics, without all the other bells and whistles, the streaming videos and the fancy flyers. In his mind, a lot of the tactics paid for by the philanthropies and implemented by the consultants were over-the-top and created a lot of controversy the project did not need.

While Jupp does not agree, Dickinson and Wissink believe the election could have been won without the campaign. Wissink remarks, "I don't think it helped as much as it could have."

Dickinson is clear on the subject as well: "Do I believe that through our normal ways of doing things we could have won? Yes!" Further, he not only questions the efficacy of the campaign but also reminds us of the damage he believes it did. "I wish we wouldn't have done it. We would have won anyway and wound up not having to pay the price." Wissink points out that when she began as president, the union had 3,200 teacher members. When she stepped down, there were only 2,800 members. Had members in fact left because of the ProComp campaign?

While some union leaders may have preferred education to advocacy and while they believe the initiative would have received their members' blessing without the campaign, others, particularly the organizers, are less sure. They also disagree with the union's decision to simply let members "just make their minds up," as Greg Ahrnsbrak says. "When a union wants a strike, they sell it. Our union rode the fence," he critiques the let-the-membership-decide strategy for advancing ProComp. "I approached this to win. That's the way I approach things. I wasn't about to waste all this time. I believed very strongly that this was the right approach to take to paying teachers. It was a win-win for everybody." Speaking plainly, Ahrnsbrak responds to the suggestion that the campaign failed to impact the election: "The campaign did impact the election and in fact made the difference in the outcome."[3]

As former Colorado Education Association president, Beverly Ausfahl reflects on the scope of the entire ProComp project and appreciates the fact that the foundations took the unusual step of working with teachers to develop a fair compensation system instead of foisting a prepackaged punitive system on them: "This wouldn't have happened without Rose because there is no development money available in Colorado school districts."[4] In this context, she believes, it is understandable that the foundations funded the campaign. Putting herself in the position of the philanthropies, she reminds us that as the vote drew nearer, there seemed to be a lot of confusion about what people were voting on and the meaning of that vote. So, she reflects, "the foundations came in and said we need to have an accurate picture of what is going on. We are putting money in to ensure [that] voters receive information and rapid answers to their questions so they can make an intelligent, informed decision."

As an outsider, Bill Slotnik believes that the union vote was won by the combination of his neutral third-party research, the opt-in feature that didn't make ProComp mandatory, changes within the district, and the foundation money. He insists: "There is no question but that the money made a difference for some, but no question that it also produced some resentment, too."[5]

Having heard concerns about many of the campaigns he and other political consulting firms have run, responding to criticism that the Pro-Comp campaign went over the top or was completely unnecessary, John Britz says that there are "more armchair quarterbacks in politics than who watch football on Sunday" and that "all campaigns have things they could do better and all campaigns have things where they hit the nail on the head." "If we would have spent so much money to the point where we had turned people off, it would have [been] reflected [in]the number we got on election day," he responds to the suggestion that the campaign engaged in overkill.[6]

Obviously, we will never know if the election would have been won without the campaign; nor will we ever know if limiting the effort to union organizing would have sufficed. Phil Gonring and Veronica Davey believe, however, that their foundations did the right thing by intervening in the process. There was more at stake, after all, than harmony within the union. The children of Denver would be better served by a compensation system that rewarded performance and helped attract and retain high quality teachers. The election carried with it historical significance as well. Without teacher approval of ProComp, as we have already made mention, teacher-compensation reform potentially would be set back for years to come. No one would have believed that an urban union would really allow such dramatic reform to happen.

In making the decision to launch the campaign, Lydia Peña, chair of the Rose Education Committee, reflects:

> The Education Committee believed that there was not really fierce opposition to ProComp; teachers were simply uninformed. ProComp was not a bad thing. If teachers really understood it, they would find it to be in their best interest. The opt-in clause allowed current teachers to stay in the existing system. No one was being forced to do anything, not even newly hired teachers who would be enrolled automatically in the new system. They could choose to work elsewhere if they did not find ProComp palatable. Had ProComp forced teachers into the new system, it is unlikely that Rose Community Foundation would have had a stomach for funding a campaign. And it is hard not to feel a bit vindicated by the numbers of teachers who have actually opted in to ProComp, including those who openly opposed it during both the union and general elections. If ProComp were a horrible thing foisted on teachers by a bunch of philanthropists, as has been suggested, then why after only two opt-in windows is 40 percent of the workforce enrolled in the new system?[7]

On the other hand, Gonring is not naive about what the foundations did. He understands that DCTA must feel a little like a political candidate running in a mainstream election who cannot control the actions of a 527 organization. Nor is he innocent of the fact that the campaign did in fact produce a divided union membership, with four in ten teachers opposing the new compensation system. These numbers would alarm any membership organization, but they especially worry a union operating in a state whose laws do not require all teachers to become members as a condition of employment.

Although he was frustrated by union leadership's decision to remain neutral and not launch a campaign, Gonring understands how ProComp flies in the face of typical union culture, so he is sympathetic toward the challenging situation in which Dickinson and Wissink found themselves. When unions strike, they typically walk out for defensive reasons; they inevitably work to ensure that their wage and benefits packages at a minimum keep pace with inflation and that work rules, like seniority privileges, remain in force. ProComp, on the other hand, is an offensive maneuver, one that gives teachers the opportunity to gain turf, not protect it. ProComp was a new idea to DCTA, in the same way that involvement in a union election was new to philanthropies.

Labor's skills at playing offense are in their early stages of development, and DCTA's involvement in ProComp should be seen in this light. Remember, virtually every teacher union in the country faced with a similar decision has said "no" to plans like ProComp. The NEA, while explicitly not opposing the Denver effort, has policy statements against similar programs. Moving from opposition to what we might call "enlightened neutrality" is clear progress, and for that progress we must thank both the union president and executive director. DCTA president Wissink constantly had to juggle the concerns of angry members on either side. In spite of that discontent, Wissink was fond of saying that she "didn't get out her union playbook" when she came to work in the morning. Had she done that, ProComp never would have happened, because the playbook does not allow for the changes to the teacher compensation system found in ProComp. Yet trouble between the union and the school district was just around the corner.

More Labor Strife

With the union election behind them, ProComp advocates may have been tempted to coast into November 2005, when Denver voters would decide the fate of ProComp with a "yes" or "no" vote on a $25 million mill levy. A far greater obstacle loomed on the horizon, however: two separate sets of salary negotiations, the first beginning in the spring of 2004, the second in 2005.

Just two months after approving ProComp, DCTA made public its unhappiness with the pay teachers were receiving under the existing salary system. Wissink stood on a table in front of the district's administration building, leading a protest against the salary offer that the district had made during that spring's negotiations. And she wrote letters chastising the school district to local newspapers, questioning the actions of the superintendent.[8] The *Denver Post* recorded board member Elaine Berman's own unhappiness with the union and its president: "We're disappointed in her tactics. . . . We feel like we've been forthright, we have provided all the information; we would like to return to the negotiating team tomorrow, but they won't until August."[9]

Finally settling in the fall of 2004 for a 1 percent increase, the union still had not regained the career earnings it believed its members lost by giving up a step the previous year. ProComp advocates feared the worst, that they were headed for another and far more acrimonious showdown in 2005, just months before the taxpayer election, when a potential work action would spill over negatively into the mill-levy campaign. Some worried that the union would leverage its demands against ProComp, subtly trying to blackmail the district into supporting its conditions and, in fact, challenging the superintendent to call its bluff. The political consultants proclaimed that if there were not a settlement in the spring of 2005, there could be no mill-levy campaign in November. Teachers fighting over salaries in the press, they suggested, would doom any attempt to raise taxes.

Acrimonious negotiations were exacerbated by the fact that the man who had been the union's chief negotiator for years, Jupp, had fallen out of favor within DCTA leadership circles and no longer worked on the bargaining team. Jupp describes himself as "being on a little dingy, floating toward administration, Captain Bly for the entire ProComp project." This Captain Bly was not involved in the 2004 settlement, nor could he help in 2005. Former superintendent Jerry Wartgow believes that this adversely affected negotiations: no one on the bargaining team had Jupp's experience with the budget, which led to constant and fruitless diversions at the bargaining table.[10]

To help secure a settlement, Rose joined DCTA and DPS in funding a $63,000 study designed to put Denver teacher pay within the context of wages paid teachers in the greater Denver metro area. RCF insisted that the report be issued jointly and that the parties agree to a release strategy; nevertheless, someone leaked to the press a draft containing errors favorable to the union. An inaccurate news article in one of the local papers and even more acrimony between the parties quickly followed. Later, when the district and union released the final authorized study, it detailed the need for an additional $4 million for DPS teacher salaries. Unfortunately, however, the school district faced a $17 million overall budget shortfall.

Despite the deficit, sometime early in the spring all sides began to believe that a settlement was possible. Preliminary estimates suggested that annual cost-of-living adjustment used by the legislature to calculate increases in K–12 funding would be high enough to pay for the salary increase demanded by teachers. Unfortunately, soon thereafter, the actual figure came in much lower, a meager 0.1 percent. The air again went out of a lot of sails. There was talk of a strike, likely in the fall. More and more, the prospect for a settlement and a mill-levy campaign seemed remote. Feeling like a long suffering hometown fan, Gonring heard again and again from administrators, "Wait 'til next year."

For the philanthropies though, there might not be a next year. The Broad Foundation and Rose placed strategic calls to Denver's mayor John Hickenlooper, DPS superintendent Wartgow, DCTA president Wissink, and school board members to remind them that a lot was riding on their ability to settle the contract dispute and that nation was watching to see whether PFP would actually be implemented in a major American city. "Get it done" was the consistent message. Further, Steve Shogan, Rose's board chair, and Gonring met with the mayor's office to ask for the popular politician's assistance with the dispute.

Wartgow reports he did feel a great deal of pressure to settle, from the mayor, from Eli Broad, and from Rose. He says he did settle to save ProComp but states emphatically, "I knew I was going to do it anyway." He had announced his retirement in February 2005 and says he did not plan to put his successor in a position to have to settle a contract at the beginning of his tenure, a situation he had faced when he was hired. In fact, he suggests that he was able to turn the tables on those who had called to pressure him. Once the campaign for the mill levy began, in fact, he asked them for either contributions or support on the campaign trail.

The sides agreed to terms on April 21, 2005. Teachers received the raise they had demanded, greater say in instructional issues, and more planning time.[11] The deal hinged on a final $180,000 the district was able to come up with through making more administrative cuts. As important, the settlement kept the mill-levy election alive because it averted a work action that would have killed off the momentum that was building for the tax increase. Both Denver dailies suggested that the settlement had in fact averted a work stoppage.[12]

$25 Million or Bust

With the spring settlement behind them, ProComp advocates began convening as "Voters for 3A," the citizens committee that would oversee the mill-levy campaign to fund ProComp. Cochaired by Elaine Berman and Colorado's Republican kingmaker and businessman Bruce Benson, the committee first met in May in Benson's oil and gas company's downtown Denver offices.

Viewing mementos in Benson's office is like gazing upon framed pictures of icons on the walls of some grand Republican pizzeria, with pictures of DiMaggio and Balboa replaced by those of Benson with some of the most powerful conservative men and women in recent history: Margaret Thatcher, Ronald Reagan, George H. W. Bush, George W. Bush, Richard Nixon, Gerald Ford, and Bob Dole. The lone democrat on display is Hickenlooper, with whom Benson worked on a major campaign to give Colorado a five-year break from its restrictive Taxpayer's Bill of Rights (TABOR). On that campaign, Benson broke ranks with the extreme fiscal conservatives in his own party.

Benson, as the Republican party's 1994 nominee for Colorado governor, past chair of the state Republican party, and veteran of numerous political campaigns in which he supported candidates most ProComp leaders worked hard to defeat, might seem an odd addition to the Pro-Comp team, but he became a huge supporter of DPS and the chairman of the DPS Foundation because of his friendship with Superintendent

Wartgow—the two were neighbors and had worked together on higher education when Wartgow oversaw the state's community-college system and Benson chaired the Colorado Commission on Higher Education. Benson had become a big fan of ProComp.

"It sounds like a Republican idea to me," he says boyishly, knowing he is being interviewed by someone who does not share his political beliefs. "It's outside the box. It's revolutionary. It's what we do in business. Somebody does a great job and you get a raise."[13]

A year earlier, Benson actually arranged for Jupp, Wartgow, Berman, and Wissink to meet with President Bush at Buckley Air Force Base outside of Denver, where the president had arrived for a fundraiser. Shortly thereafter, driving in a limousine with the president, Benson discussed the initiative with him, and he received it positively, Benson reports. In Denver, however, one does not need Republican credentials to win an election. In fact, polling data showed that involving Colorado's conservative Governor Bill Owens in the 3A campaign would actually have cost the effort votes. No, what Benson brought to the campaign was his irreplaceable political savvy—along with his and his friends' money.

His counsel and clout were important in keeping the November ballot clear of other tax initiatives. Working with Berman and others on the committee, he made it clear to early-childhood advocates that despite the worthiness of their cause, their suggestion to connect ProComp with a tax for preschool education was too risky. He feared that with too many tax issues on the ballot, voters would just check "no" on everything. Further, his depth of experience working with political consultants balanced the inexperience of people like Gonring and Jupp, whom he counseled, "You worry too much. We're going to win."

It eventually helped the campaign that the new DPS superintendent, Michael Bennet, who started in June 2005, had significant political experience as the mayor's chief of staff. Overseeing the campaign was Greg Kolomitz, a veteran of several school-district elections and most recently the campaign director for Bill Ritter, elected as governor of Colorado in November of 2006. He would be joined by Welchert and Britz, who managed direct mail and grass root components of the 3A campaign and other political consultants who continue to work on statewide campaigns. Our point here is that ProComp's future had been turned over to some of Colorado's most successful political operatives.

At early meetings of the campaign, the citizens committee unpacked polling data and the issues the campaign would have to consider. First, polling data suggested that the initiative would pass by a small margin, putting it at risk to organized opposition. Second, ProComp was vulnerable because there was something in it for both Democratic and Republican voters to hate. Polling showed that Denver Democrats liked the notion of paying teachers more but did not take kindly to the notion of tying pay to test scores. Conservative voters did not like raising taxes, but they relished the prospect of tying pay to student learning. Further, ProComp was just too complicated for the average voter to understand. In fact, an early survey of registered voters found that the more they learned about ProComp over the course of an interview, the less they liked it. Finally, the campaign's biggest obstacle was the longstanding voter belief that DPS did not spend taxpayer dollars wisely, a concern likely exacerbated by news stories that the district had not been using the 2003 mill-levy moneys as promised. All of these concerns had to be addressed in the campaign.

However, there was an overarching pragmatic issue, which would have an impact on what needed to take place before the campaign could begin. This had to do with the creation of the ballot language. Rich Allen, DPS's assistant superintendent of budget and finance, and Jupp knew from their financial projection work with the JTF that ProComp could not stay fiscally viable over time using the traditional mill-levy framework. Because the traditional framework asks voters to approve a flat dollar amount, and teacher salaries must be adjusted for inflation, ProComp was destined for eventual bankruptcy. As a result, Jupp and Allen pushed the campaign to create ballot language that would allow the $25 million to keep pace with inflation.

This, of course, was not received favorably by people who wanted to win, including the political consultants who feared that voters would balk at such a measure. It led to several meetings in which committee members floated various options, such as the requiring voters to reauthorize ProComp in a later election, a possibility unacceptable to a union leadership that had promised its members it would support ProComp only if it were financially sustainable. Another election would put that sustainability at risk.

With strong endorsements from Bruce Benson, Elaine Berman, and Les Woodward, Allen's argument about inflation adjustments won the day. The group received help from an attorney who volunteered for the campaign and found that there was in fact precedence for an adjusted mill levy in Colorado; nevertheless, he let the committee know that the ballot language could in fact be challenged during the waiting period between filing and certification, as required by law. There was then no case law indicating which way a court might rule. The only previous example had been challenged; however, the court had ruled on a procedural rather than a substantive matter. But what would an election be without obstacles? At this point, after overcoming so many other challenges, ProComp leaders were worried but confident.

Fortunately, no one challenged the language during the waiting period. Perhaps, again, this was a matter of pure dumb luck, as the state's antitax advocates were otherwise preoccupied trying to defeat ballot measures (Referenda C and D) that would suspend refunds from the state's taxpayers bill of rights (TABOR) for five years. In fact, Benson believes that the millions of dollars spent on campaigns for and against Referenda C and D kept those who would oppose ProComp from paying attention to the ballot language and the 3A election.

Buoyed by its success in getting the language on the ballot, the campaign attended to the other necessary issues. With $250,000 contributions from Rose and the Gary Williams Energy Corporation and $100,000 personal contributions from Benson and Eli Broad, the committee—and principally Benson, Berman, and Bennet—was well on its way to raising what would become a $1.3 million war chest, the largest campaign budget for a mill levy in Colorado history.

It is important to note here that Rose is a public charity, not a private foundation. Therefore, it can in fact make political contributions, as long as they are not for candidates or political parties. However, the unprecedented size of the contribution is noteworthy, since it constituted nearly 20 percent of the entire campaign budget. Rose president

Sheila Bugdanowitz reflects on the out-of-the-ordinary gift: "The trustees knew the foundation had driven this initiative and felt enormous responsibility for its success. They understood that the private foundation participants couldn't financially support the campaign and that the responsibility fell on them. They were institutionally committed to passing the mill levy."[14]

The contributions allowed for a large television-advertising blitz. Eventually, two commercials would air, the first contrasting the wages of teachers with those of baseball players, professional golfers, and entertainers—capitalizing on polling data suggesting that voters really do believe that educators are underpaid. The second, aimed at addressing voter distrust of the school district, portrayed Denver's popular Mayor Hickenlooper with DPS's new superintendent, Bennet, telling Denver voters that the school district could in fact be trusted with their money.

Beyond television, several pieces of direct mail went out to likely voters, including one featuring the mayor eating lunch with a group of students. Careful to avoid playing to liberal fears that pay would be based on standardized tests, the mailings also focused on other components of the system. Separate mailings detailing the standardized test components were sent out to Republican voters. Jay Rust, one of the super-organizers from the union campaign, oversaw efforts to encourage voting, which involved distributing yard signs and coordinating neighborhood walks with teachers and other volunteers, including advocacy groups like Great Education Colorado and Northwest Parents for Excellent schools. Rose's Bugdanowitz and Shogan knocked on doors of undecided voters. The campaign also organized a speakers' bureau, scheduling speaking engagements for board members—Bennet, Jupp, Gonring, and others—who spoke to groups of influential citizens, realtor associations, the Denver Chamber of Commerce, neighborhood associations, activist organizations, rotaries, and numerous others. At the urging of the campaign, U.S. senator Ken Salazar endorsed 3A at a press conference in a park across the street from the high school his daughter attended, announcing, "This is really an historic effort on the part of education. It gives us the opportunity to recruit and retain the best."[15] In addition, the campaign made robo calls to likely voters, with recordings of both the mayor and Wissink asking them to support ProComp.

The campaign had worried about opposition, especially among teachers, but it materialized late in the game and, although opponents held a press conference and generated a couple of news stories, they never gathered real momentum. Teacher volunteers for the "Vote No on 3A" campaign lined the medians of some of Denver's busiest streets with home made anti 3A signs. One of the opponents, a longtime Denver teacher, appeared on Colorado Public Radio's *Colorado Matters* public affairs program and suggested that ProComp only had been developed because Rose was trying to destroy the union. While some who had heard the program—including Gonring's sister—commented to him that the teacher's concerns made them think twice about 3A, he was persuaded by seasoned campaigners like Benson that it would make very little difference in the outcome of the election.

After positive editorials in both newspapers, the *Rocky Mountain News* ran a column by an influential local conservative talk-show host, Mike Rosen, in which he argued that the people of Denver should vote against the tax increase. Again, inexperienced campaigners were assured that the people of Denver, a Democratic enclave, would not pay attention to his views the way someone living in one of the city's conservative suburbs would.

Whatever concerns Denver voters might have had, these were assuaged by a $1.3 million campaign that was as convincing as it was overwhelming. On November 1, 2005, Denver voters gave their seal of approval to an effort that had officially begun six years earlier, endorsing the new system 58 percent to 42 percent, a figure that remarkably mirrored the teacher vote. Of the victory, Kolomitz says, "We won because we spent a lot of money and there wasn't any credible organized opposition."[16] That night, Hickenlooper and Bennet, his former chief-of-staff turned superintendent, stood atop the bar at Denver's Trinity Grille, addressing cheering supporters and thanking them for their work. Indeed, ProComp had moved out of the skunk works and survived neglect and labor strife. It had spanned the terms of six superintendents, sometimes surviving on life support, rarely the darling of anyone. Yet now it was the property of the mayor, a brand new superintendent, and the people of Denver.

After the victory party, Gonring and Jupp celebrated over dinner with a few of those who had labored to keep ProComp alive. They were pleased, to be sure. But they had expected to feel ecstatic, and they were struck by the modesty of their joy. They realized that while the campaign was not a walk in the park, ProComp had overcome far greater obstacles: the vote over the length of the pilot, the union ProComp election, and 2005's labor strife. 3A's victory was in fact a bit anticlimactic. They also saw that for the previous few months shoulders a lot larger than their own had been carrying the project—those of the mayor, the superintendent, Benson, Berman, Woodward, and some of Colorado's best political consultants. The era of individual entrepreneurialism was over. It was time for the heavy lifting of policy implementation to begin.

6

Implementing ProComp

We Did What?

"No company in the world would have attempted to do what
we have done, at a time when we are reducing the budget 15–
20 percent."

—Andre Pettigrew, DPS assistant superintendent
and ProComp transition team member, 2006

On November 2, 2005, just hours after citizens of Denver approved the mill levy, Jeff Buck became the Neil Armstrong of ProComp, taking a giant step for his colleagues and signing up for the new system. When the authors later found out Buck was the first to enroll, they contacted him for a response: "Yes, it is true. I opted-in online in my office the morning after the election. I meant to do it at home before I came in to make sure I was first, but I'm not much of a morning person and I spaced it. We were out past my 9:30 bedtime at the election celebration the night before. I was on the Joint Taskforce that designed this thing so I figured I'd better put my money where my mouth is. How could anyone take it seriously if the architects of the program didn't join?"[1]

Over the next 54 days of the first opt-in window, more than 780 teachers would walk on the moon with Buck, permanently leaving the single salary schedule behind. The number of pioneers far exceeded the expectations of even the greatest optimist, Connie White, who had projected 700. Most had guessed that about 200 would take advantage of the first chance to opt in.

As of November 1, 2006, some 1,650 of 4,200 DPS teachers have become ProComp members, representing about 41 percent of all current DPS teachers. Of these 1,650 participants, 535 were hired after December 31, 2005 and had no choice but to be enrolled in the new salary system. The other 1,115, nearly 30 percent of the workforce, made the choice to join ProComp, a remarkable figure given that 41 percent of union members had voted against the reform in 2004.

While Buck was intimately familiar with ProComp and did not need any additional information to inform his decision, many of those teachers who followed him were eager for information. To educate the first group of interested teachers, the ProComp team held face-to-face discussions to explain each teacher's specific salary situation. To make the workload manageable, the district hired and trained retired DPS teachers to conduct salary discussions with their former colleagues. With compensation now tied to various aspects of teacher knowledge and skills, market incentives, professional evaluation, and student growth, the issues for individual teachers are complicated. Using a salary calculator developed during the research and development phase of ProComp, teachers were able determine whether they would fare better or worse under ProComp, and the specific point in their careers at which it would make most sense for them to join.

As measured by such enthusiastic teacher participation, ProComp is off to an excellent start. The success of establishing ProComp in the first place and its fast start are major accomplishments that appropriately have captured national media attention. But the story would be incomplete if we did not address what happened when ProComp moved from the entrepreneurial, against-the-odds idea phase to the heavy-lifting stage of policy implementation, a critical juncture in any entrepreneurial venture. The business literature on entrepreneurship often focuses on the question of whether the leaders of the entrepreneurial start-up phase are the appropriate people to develop and oversee a full-fledged organization as it grows, and as issues of management supercede the importance of ideas. But the opposite side of this tension is the possibility that the entrepreneurial venture will flounder, once it is removed from the nurturing hands of the key entrepreneurs. In the case of ProComp, one of the central entrepreneurs, Brad Jupp, has moved from shepherding the reform as a union leader to overseeing it as the senior academic policy advisor to Denver's new superintendent Michael Bennet. Phil Gonring continues his involvement in ProComp from the outside, as Rose continues to make grants in support of the new salary system to the school district.

Getting ProComp to the point where teachers could actually sign up for it required endurance, tenacity, and good luck; yet the implementation of the new pay system has been no simple task either, demanding patience, creativity, and even more tenacity. In part, the difficulty comes because ProComp is not the simple system Irv Moskowitz envisioned back in 1998. The district now bases teacher pay on far more variables than the traditional steps and lanes of the single salary schedule or the objective-setting process imagined by 1999's Board of Education. Difficulties implementing the complex system have been further exacerbated by the severe budget shortfalls DPS continues to face. The administrative units responsible for building the systems to make ProComp work—human resources, Departments of Technology Systems, and others—have all been faced with 15 percent budget cuts for each of the past four years. As Chief Operating Officer Andre Pettigrew notes, DPS was putting ProComp into practice not only "on a shoestring," but "on a shoestring that was being cut shorter every year."[2] Losing financial resources made maintaining momentum difficult enough, but the loss of important personnel meant that key elements of institutional learning were lost as well.

Implementation generally is a critical stage in any public policy, indeed perhaps *the* critical stage. A great policy idea poorly implemented will not be long remembered as a success, as Pressman and Wildavsky presciently suggested in the deliberately long title of their 1966 classic: *Implementation: How Great Expectations in Washington Are Dashed in Oakland; or, Why It's Amazing That Federal Programs Work at All, This Being a Saga . . . of Ruined Hopes."* All of the key supporters of ProComp want it to succeed and to see it through its substantial challenges in the implementation stage. They know, like all policy initiatives, ProComp could become yet another saga of ruined hopes if people stop paying attention to it.

In this chapter, then, we first explore the nuts-and-bolts implementation challenges surrounding ProComp and how they have been addressed. Then, we turn to the mechanisms in place to evaluate ProComp to ensure that it is accountable to its purposes and is revised as necessary to ensure maximum effectiveness. Finally, we link to our previous discussions of key institutional players in the development of ProComp by considering the ongoing roles of the union and philanthropy—even as the essential focus of ProComp moves primarily within the DPS administrative structures.

"What Do You Mean, ProComp Is Not Our First Priority?"

While ProComp is a signature and important innovation for DPS, the school district, like those in most of America's cities, faces many other challenges as it endeavors to educate more than 60,000 students each day. These include low levels of state financing, an increasing percentage of students who are at risk or who need significant language training, loss of students and per-student funding to charter and other choice schools, and the need to address NCLB legislation. In all the district does, it must confront the chronic underachievement of its students.

So while both those inside and outside the school district point to ProComp as a signature program within DPS, they know that it cannot be the engine that drives the train. In fact, Jupp likes to say that ProComp is the servant to the district's broader initiatives, ones currently defined by the comprehensive *Denver Plan* masterminded by Superintendent Bennet, and developed with both teachers and administrators, including ProComp leaders Connie White and Shirley Scott. In fact, the plan, which will guide instructional reform in the school district for the foreseeable future, never mentions ProComp, although it will soon become clear how the new teacher pay system supports *The Denver Plan*. Spanning 92 pages, the tome, which the district calls a living document that is subject to change, enumerates key goals, objectives, activities, time frames, outcomes, and measurements. Among many other charges, *The Denver Plan* calls for the development of a highly trained teaching corps and "a coherent instructional reform plan" that will "set high academic expectations for all students and align curriculum, instruction, assessment, and professional development to Colorado's defined state standards and college entrance requirements."[3]

Aligning ProComp to the Denver Plan is one of the key challenges facing the ProComp Management Team, although making the connections between many of the goals and components of the Plan and ProComp is not difficult. ProComp's PDUs, for instance, will become a tool to create the highly trained faculty demanded in *The Denver Plan* and teachers will use the assessments developed by the school district in the student-growth objective-setting process.

Management Structure

That *The Denver Plan* never mentions ProComp may make our readers think that nothing has changed since the PFP pilot was relegated to a skunk works within DPS. Nothing could be further from the truth; while it serves in a supporting role to the district's broader initiatives, ProComp remains a high priority for DPS, as the district institutionalizes the new salary system in a transition period that will run through 2008. Following the successful union election in March of 2004, Jerry Wartgow and Becky Wissink established the ProComp transition team as the work group within DPS responsible for the implementation of ProComp. Wartgow gave the transition team, consisting of five high-level administrators and five teachers, the authority to marshal district resources to make ProComp successful. Central administrators who had reserved judgment on whether ProComp would ever be implemented now had to make it work, as their bosses occupied positions on the transition team. ProComp developed what Pettigrew calls "executive sponsorship," as the heads of various departments returned from team meetings to their separate units with lists of what needed to be done to advance the compensation reform; those units were then required to implement ProComp without the inertia or opposition that were present during the pilot.

After the election, the transition team established 14 separate working groups, a number that it whittled down to four in 2006. High-level assistant superintendents, such as Pettigrew, no longer sit on the group because it is no longer necessary to signal to DPS staff that ProComp is important. Pettigrew has been replaced by Ed Freeman, director of technology services, a man who is regularly in the trenches of ProComp implementation and who has more direct knowledge of what is actually happening on the ground.

Currently the transition team oversees the operations of four work groups, which are in turn supported by district staff, some of whom have their salaries paid for by Rose grants, others by district general operating funds. While in November of 2006 momentum is building to maintain some ProComp staff positions and a remnant of the Transition Team well into the future, designated ProComp staff positions currently are slated to be phased out at the end of the 2007–08 school year—with the transition team itself scheduled to dissolve in 2013, when the current ProComp Agreement expires. Transition team cochair White notes: "This is a hand-off plan for ProComp to live within the DPS departments."[4]

In short, no single guru or czar within DPS will oversee all aspects of ProComp. Already leaders within Chief Academic Officer Jaime Aquino's teaching and learning and leadership development units oversee key components of the reform, with Maureen Sanders, the executive director of leadership and development, managing PDU development and Shirley Scott administering student-growth objectives. And professional evaluation currently has its home in the human resources department. Indeed, over the next two years, integration will become the rule as ProComp stops being a stand-alone reform, and as administrators in curriculum and assessment departments and principals and their supervisors incorporate ProComp into their daily activities.

Before final integration can occur, however, the transition team has its work cut out for it overseeing the efforts of the four work groups. The first group has responsibility for the implementation of the student growth initiative, professional development unit, and professional-evaluation components of ProComp, while the second focuses on the logistics of tuition reimbursement, payroll opt-in procedures, initial placement, advanced degrees, and licenses. A third work group manages the implementation of the market-incentive, CSAP-expectations, and distinguished-school components of the new salary system, while a final group oversees the evaluation of ProComp and the professional review panel, the body of teachers and principals charged with resolving disputes in the place of lawyers, human resources specialists, and union professionals. Institutionalizing the partnership between labor and management, each group has both teacher and administrative leaders, as well as members from both groups.

In 2006–08, the work groups had to accomplish an array of complex tasks, though the primary task of the first work group deserves special mention. Work-group one's main focus is to take specific ProComp elements through several generations of development. For instance, based on what it learned during the pilot implementation of PDUs at the end of the 2005–06 school year, the work group will make revisions to the process, test those revisions in 2006–07 and then make further revisions in 2007–08. This illustrates the important point that more than seven years after the pilot began, DPS is still engaged in research and development, something Pettigrew emphasizes by reminding us that "venture capital [philanthropy] provides R&D capacity in the DPS system that doesn't exist anywhere else." The work groups and the Transition Team will also propose changes to the ProComp Agreement as the project unfolds. For instance, to prevent the work-flow surge that occurs in a short opt-in period and to give greater flexibility to teachers, union members recently voted to change the window from a few weeks to almost the entire school year.

It would be inappropriate to end this section on ProComp management without some discussion of the current role of the superintendent. The key players behind ProComp refused to let both the pilot and implementation efforts fail despite dizzying changes in the superintendence, a rate of change that was even faster than the velocity at which a typical urban school district churns top executives. The full development of ProComp spanned the terms of six superintendents: Irv Moskowitz (1994–99), Sharon Johnson (interim 1999), Chip Zullinger (1999–2000), Bernadette Seick (interim 2000–01), Jerry Wartgow (2001–05), and now Michael Bennet (2005–present). While ProComp in its earliest stages could survive while ignored in the skunk works, it would not thrive in this transition period if the current superintendent were not engaged. When Bennet became superintendent in 2005, he maintained the same focus on ProComp that his predecessor had fostered and campaigned vigorously for the November 2005 mill-levy override. Indeed, Bennet's appointment of Jupp as senior academic policy advisor signaled to all how important he believed ProComp to be. In a district environment that is highly sensitive to even the most subtle changes in direction, administrators likely would have backed off ProComp implementation if Bennet appeared disinterested in it. Administrators and teachers clearly know that ProComp is a central part of DPS plans, even as they struggle with its implementation challenges—and its challenges are many.

"It's the Technology, Stupid"

Clearly the greatest challenge confronting the transition team is the amount of work it must accomplish before the end of the transition period, particularly the first work group, which must test and revise key components of the new system. However, because they are significant, we also must focus on the challenges technology presents to ProComp's success. In any given year, for instance, a ProComp teacher may set objectives, undergo an evaluation, pursue a PDU, teach a grade level that is assessed by the state, pursue a market incentive, and teach in a distinguished school. All the information pertaining to that teacher and her involvement in these six ProComp components must be stored somewhere and then reported to payroll, sometimes monthly. Can you imagine what would happen if administrators had to do all this by hand?

From the perspective of the teacher, however, the single act of setting a student-growth objective is a complex activity requiring her to access web sites and databases, including those that store her students' achievement histories. Unfortunately, integrated web-based applications to make life easier for both administrators and teachers do not yet exist. The need for web-based systems to support teachers, principals, and school supervisors in the objective setting process became clear during the PFP pilot program.

Jupp recalls that during the pilot, the design team learned the value of web-based work-flow management systems that would reduce paperwork and allow teachers and administrators to maximize the time they spent talking about outcomes for students as they set student-growth objectives. The "great evil" the design team was trying to avoid was teachers having to shuffle three or four pages back and forth to and from their principal, who then had to make sophisticated judgments about a set of papers submitted by 20 to 40 teachers before making copies for her own supervisor to review. It was only a small improvement giving the teacher multiple online systems to toggle back and forth between as she set the objectives, accessed student-achievement data, and examined school-improvement plans. Pilot leaders took that learning to the transition team years later as Jupp and his colleagues envisioned a more comprehensive database that integrated certain vital functions in school-performance management, like school-improvement planning and the three key elements of ProComp: PDUs, teacher evaluation, and student-growth objectives.

The district IT department discovered that making such a broad and unifying system, especially one that stored data over multiple years, was a much more difficult task than originally imagined. In fact, technology managers came to realize that the web-based systems they had were a combination of one-off data collection systems that the district had invested in over many years. As a result, those systems would never be able communicate with each other. They also found, to their disappointment, that venders were not interested in helping them create an integrated system that would work for ProComp specifically, preferring instead to sell standardized products that were not tailored to any district's unique needs.

These challenges could not stop the transition team, however. In fact, it has developed a web-based work-flow management system that allows teachers to access student-achievement data and their own student-growth objectives over time, all from the same platform. Further, the system allows principals to check on the status of all their teachers' objectives and lets district administrators examine the quality of objectives in schools they supervise. Similar web-based work-flow management systems are under development for the PDU and professional evaluation components of ProComp and should be up and running by the end of the 2007–08 school year.

All of the systems, however, will someday need to be able to interact with the payroll department so that accurate paychecks can be cut without error and a lot of staff time. Currently, this is not always possible. As an example, the Department of Student Services in DPS houses all the information on nurses and other health professionals in a database that is not connected to payroll. As might be expected, there have been a handful of mistakes as checks have gone out the door during the first few months of ProComp implementation. Facing this challenge head-on, the transition team has taken the remarkable step of contacting by phone or meeting individually with every teacher who had received an overpayment check, not only to apologize but to assure her that the error will not occur in the future.

So the challenges of work-flow management and the absence of integrated systems that cross numerous departments loom large. It is unlikely and potentially impossible for the district to provide a single unifying technology system. Instead, the district has what Jupp calls "the green piece of Lego" that connects other Legos on the same platform. The web-based work-flow management system for the student-growth component now connects to live student-growth and human-resources data. Once the work-flow components for PDUs and the comprehensive professional evaluation element are developed, they will join student growth on the same platform. Outcomes will be reported online to human resources and payroll. At the end of the transition period, the school district will have a comprehensive data system that unites several better designed strategic systems that are able to communicate with each other. This will be a major triumph.

Technology is at the root of another challenge confronting DPS, as the cultural and linguistic differences between teachers and the self-described "geeks" play themselves out. As Freeman, technology services director quips, "Techies speak Klingon while people in instruction speak English."[5] Pettigrew simply asks, "How do you translate human behavior into zeroes and ones so a computer can get it done?" And so it is that teachers and administrators with backgrounds in education report that in their work groups they sometimes receive reports written in nomenclature unfamiliar to them. Techies feel the same way: workers in technology departments did not understand, for instance, that what educators were calling "a teacher assignment" could in fact be a nurse, a social worker, or a counselor.

ProComp has, by necessity, stimulated conversations across various departments, cross-talk that has been transformational for DPS. Staff reports that the exchanges have had positive spillovers into other DPS policies and programs, as the limited fiscal resources for implementation have forced and promoted teamwork among transition team members and technology specialists who must work together. In meeting with the lead technical staff and educators, Paul Teske and Gonring not only witnessed firsthand the linguistic differences among the parties but also found the friendships among them to be palpable. When asked why they have been so successful in a resource-poor environment, one of the technical staff remarked, "Everyone at this table is as stubborn as all get-out and we refuse to let it [ProComp] fail."[6]

With strong leadership at the top and stubborn workers implementing ProComp in the field, it is a certainty that ProComp is here to stay. With that in mind, we now turn to ensuring its quality and success over time.

Accountability on Steroids

Shortly after ProComp's passage, *Freakonomics*' coauthor, esteemed economist Steven Levitt, spoke at a luncheon in downtown Denver. Fans of that book, like one of the authors of this one— who played hooky from work because he could not put the work down—will remember the fun and interesting chapter entitled, "What Do Schoolteachers and Sumo Wrestlers Have in Common?" And they will remember the answer to that question: some in both groups cheat.

In *Freakonomics*, Levitt and his coauthor, Stephen J. Dubner, share findings conservatively estimating that 5 percent of Chicago teachers cheat when their students take high-stakes tests, no doubt because the results of the tests reflect onto the teacher.[7] While in Denver, Levitt praised the development of ProComp but warned his audience that financial incentive systems have a tendency to become entitlements. In the administration of ProComp, administrators would need to take great care to ensure that the new salary system maintained its integrity over time and did what the framers of the plan intended it to do.[8]

In his best seller and his remarks to the citizens of Denver, Levitt frames for us some of the challenges that ProComp presents as it unfolds now and 10 and even 20 years into the future. Everyone involved in ProComp's creation and implementation wants the results promised Denver voters when they agreed to raise their taxes by $25 million a year. No one hopes ProComp or portions of it become entitlements, and leaders are well aware that every salary decision in ProComp constitutes a significant outlay of taxpayer dollars over time. PDUs provide an excellent example. At the time of the 2005 mill levy, the theoretical successful completion of a PDU equaled a $667 raise in the year the teacher completed the unit. Over time, however, that single raise grows into a much larger chunk of that teacher's career earnings. If the teacher in question works in the district 15 more years, that single successful unit results in over $10,000 of career earnings, or, seen another way, in the expense of over $10,000 of local taxes. If we assume that the trade-off for higher teacher salaries is increased accountability, then the public should expect that the PDUs will be rigorous and rigorously assessed. Denver taxpayers should be assured that only teachers who complete their proposed scope of work and in fact demonstrate they have acquired new knowledge and skills should receive a pay increase.

PDUs are not the only element of ProComp for which great accountability will be required. A thoughtful taxpayer might ask questions of other components: "Will teachers and principals write rigorous student-growth objectives so that when teachers meet them they have really accomplished a goal that merits a raise? Are ProComp bonuses being paid to teachers who really produce results? Will there be a way to catch a teacher if she alters the answers on her students' state assessment tests?" We could pose many other questions here. But the gist of our argument is clear: it will take effort to ensure that taxpayers are getting what they paid for when they took the unusual step of raising their taxes $25 million to support ProComp. It will take diligence to ensure that ProComp does not become a system of entitlements and continues to provide teachers with incentives to produce results.

Evaluation and Feedback

Fortunately, ProComp framers anticipated these challenges by institutionalizing evaluation in the ProComp Agreement. As discussed, a work group of the transition team will oversee annual internal assessments that will be reviewed by the Board of Education and DCTA's board of directors, evaluations that should address many of the questions raised in the above paragraphs. In 2009, a comprehensive third-party evaluation, which will certainly address many of the same queries, will also be presented to both boards, although as of November 2006 the evaluation had yet to be designed.

As part of the internal evaluation, the work group charged with program evaluation will regularly survey teachers and administrators to assess the quality of ProComp administration from their perspectives. But DPS has also contracted with the Piton Foundation, a local operating foundation, to conduct key components of the internal evaluation to extend both the reach and the intensity of the evaluation. While overall project management will be provided by Research Officer Pam Buckley, Piton has in turn contracted with Ed Wiley, a professor at the University of Colorado, who will act as the principal investigator. In addition to projecting the trust fund's solvency over time given current pay out rates for each of the salary system's elements, he will examine both ProComp's processes and the results those processes produce.

In the quantitative realm of the study, Wiley will assess data linking ProComp's implementation to student achievement, although a comprehensive study of its full impact on student achievement will have to unfold over a longer period of time. Nevertheless, Wiley and the Piton Foundation will be able to connect student-achievement results to specific components of ProComp immediately. For instance, data should help determine whether there is any evidence to suggest that teachers who have advanced degrees or certificates produce better student-achievement results than others. Furthermore, the study will also examine whether teachers who produce the greatest student-achievement outcomes take advantage of the market incentives and move to hard-to-staff schools, or if ProComp provides incentives for ineffective teachers to stay in hard-to-staff schools in which great teaching is especially necessary.

In addition to student-achievement information, Wiley's studies will produce evidence of the impact ProComp has on teacher recruitment and retention, and potentially upon teacher knowledge and skill. As CTAC did during the pilot, Wiley's study will also rate the quality of student-growth objectives and illuminate for the transition team the practices leading to the development of either strong or weak objectives. Finally, examining whether the theory that led to the component's inclusion in ProComp holds true, Wiley will see if the completion of PDUs leads to changes in classroom practice and ultimately to improved student learning.

Most importantly, however, Wiley's study will provide formative evaluation feedback for improvement in ProComp implementation. If he finds, for instance, that the objective-setting process needs to be changed, he may propose a specific type of training for principals. If the study shows that there is not enough oversight and guidance in the development and implementation of PDUs, Wiley may propose that the district provide additional training to reviewers, while simultaneously improving oversight of their work.

While these are only hypothetical examples, they illustrate a theme that runs throughout the story of ProComp's development: DPS and DCTA's commitment to the theory of learning that MacArthur Foundation program officer Peter Martinez proposed back in 1999 and that we first discussed in chapter 3. The union and school district continue their commitment to this theory and, we are convinced, will make changes to both ProComp's processes and the system itself, as allowed by the ProComp Agreement and the language of the mill levy. If there is not rigor, if an element of ProComp is not working, then the parties remain committed to making changes. Seen another way, the theory of learning is really a pledge made by government to be accountable to the public, as the results of these studies will annually be reported to the Board of Education and, as a result, reviewed by the press.

School reformers, school district personnel, and the general public may also find it remarkable that DPS is able to let this theory of learning flourish in an era of diminishing resources. However large portions of the tab for year one's internal evaluation are being picked up by the Piton Foundation and the University of Colorado, which has contributed much of Wiley's time. And there is no guarantee that these funding sources will continue to be available or that the school district itself, with its own resources, will develop the capacity and expertise for the level of analysis that is typically performed by scholars at top universities, like Ed Wiley. While it is likely that trust fund resources can and will be used for the external evaluation of ProComp, matters of the internal evaluation's future funding remain somewhat unsettled. In the short term, however, funding has been sought from a variety of sources, and Piton will likely continue to support the effort, at least in the second year. Monies from the federal Teacher Incentive Fund might be helpful here in the short term as well. However, such hopes need to be tempered by the reality that confronts government as it implements policy over time. As we mentioned earlier, sometimes entrepreneurial ventures flounder once the nurturing hands of the key entrepreneurs and implementers are no longer there to massage the efforts.

Future Oversight and Nurturing

Sometime soon, those who loved ProComp and willed it into policy will take other jobs, retire, develop new passions and interests, or simply get sick of the thing. The philanthropies' staffs and boards will change composition. Superintendents and mayors will come and go. The Board of Education will change membership repeatedly. Who knows, the board someday might come under the control of single-issue zealots who care only for their issue—whatever it might be.

In any event, at some point in the not-so-distant future, ProComp will be overseen by bureaucrats, board members, and union leaders who do not have the same psychological investment as those currently in office. For them, ProComp will simply be another administrative task, like making sure the busses run on time or enough teachers are hired before the start of the school year. At still another point the philanthropies will consider ProComp "that program" supported years ago by another board, another education committee, another program officer. As is human nature, there will be new ideas owned by new boards and program officers who will potentially see ProComp's future challenges as a reason to abandon the program altogether as opposed to a call to action.

Indeed, as those who nurtured ProComp go on to other endeavors, Levitt's warning should reach the volume of a screech. Instead of plugging their ears against the noise, how can those currently leading ProComp's charge protect and advance the policy by ensuring its success and its continued congruence with the wishes taxpayers expressed November 1, 2005?

This is actually a complex question that key ProComp actors may answer differently, depending on their vantage points. As the superintendent's senior academic policy advisor, Jupp is now a member of a team responsible annually for nearly $550 million of taxpayer revenue, of which the $25 million reserved for ProComp is a very small chunk. Moreover, as we already mentioned, ProComp is the servant of the school district's broader reforms, for which district administrators are directly accountable too. Given its place in the budget and that it is only one of a number of district initiatives, the level of accountability established for ProComp is remarkable. It is not unreasonable to argue that in a well-functioning school district the Board of Education should do little more than hold the superintendent and his staff accountable for outcomes for all initiatives, including implementation of the new salary system. In the high-functioning urban school district that DPS aims to be, ProComp would be in good hands, with current and future boards of education relentlessly pursuing rigor in the application of all its programs, including ProComp.

The vantage point from philanthropy may be a little different. In the case of ProComp, several foundations share responsibility for the existence of a $25 million tax. While they certainly want to see the other $550 million spent well in the broadest sense, they did not help create the mechanisms that supply these larger sets of funds or advocate that they be spent a specific way. The Rose Community Foundation alone has invested more than $4 million in the development of the new teacher pay policy, which includes a $250,000 campaign contribution to convince Denver voters to raise their taxes. Each year, the mortgage payments of Denver property owners will increase because of ProComp, and that increase will be explicitly visible on the annual tax statements received from the city, a fact that makes mill-levy taxes much more palpable to the citizens of Denver than the other levies they pay in support of public education—through state and federal taxes. In short, there is good reason to assume that taxpayers will remember those who asked them to raise their taxes, among them Rose.

In a very real sense, then, it is easy to see how the public might want to hold the foundation community accountable for ProComp. To date, some of the philanthropies have acknowledged that responsibility by continuing to support the implementation of the new system. The role they should play over time—especially in helping ensure the rigorous application of ProComp in the years, and maybe even generations, to come—should be a cause for reflection. In fact, Rose's education committee already has had preliminary discussions about how it will institutionalize an ongoing commitment to secure ProComp's success beyond the tenure of its current board and staff, but it is too early to tell what form that commitment will take. Likely, it will simply mean paying attention, remaining vigilant and flexible, and making tactical investments to ensure that the district administers ProComp rigorously and that the union and Board of Education respond appropriately to evaluators of the new salary system.

And the union has still an entirely different vantage point on ProComp's future. It will play a crucial role in the future success of ProComp, as it did in its development. We have to remember that the union kept the PFP pilot alive in its first years and that Jupp only until recently was working for the union. The current DCTA union president, Kim Ur-setta, remains steadfast in her commitment to the theory of learning that grounds the pilot: collecting data, having careful conversations, and making revisions to the system as research suggests and as allowed by the ProComp Agreement. But she is not naive and is also aware that the level of accountability attending the project may eventually put pres-sure on the union to make a difficult decision, say, for instance, if a com-ponent of ProComp popular with teachers proves not to be working. "I don't think we'd be afraid of having that conversation, if there were a need to, but it will be a difficult one," Ursetta reminds us.[9]

She also understands the dynamics of school district and union lead-ership as they may affect ProComp and says, "You never know who the next district leader is going to be—or the next union leader—and that's why unions believe in negotiated language, so no matter who's in charge the language is still there." The union leader provides fair warn-ing that at some point Denver's PFP system may need the protection the written ProComp Agreement provides.

Yet Denver voters should feel quite content about the level of ac-countability government has imposed on itself in the short term, with a negotiated agreement that requires evaluations through 2013, when it is hoped that the now separate ProComp Agreement will become part of the district's Master Agreement with teachers. But that agreement will likely not be negotiated by Jupp or Bennet on the school district's side, nor by Bruce Dickinson or Kim Ursetta on the union's side. Nor will any single board member serving when the mill levy passed be in office when the negotiations occur.

We do not know what the labor climate will be like in 2013 and sub-sequent years nor how the climate will affect ProComp. Will the par-ties maintain their commitment to the omnipresent theory of learning, making revisions to the salary system even if they anger some teachers? No doubt the current administration and the Board of Education will do everything they can to ensure that people and processes are in place to make ProComp a lasting success. There is no question that current union leadership is committed to making ProComp work for teachers over time. How the relationships among philanthropy, the school district and the union unfold in the coming years will be interesting to watch. Let us hope they develop within the context of a commitment to learning that transcends the current generation of ProComp entrepreneurs, implementers, and overseers.

7

Lessons Learned

Adapt or Die?

A ny long tale of policy development—whether it involves intra-state trucking regulations, waste-disposal zoning, or teacher pay—should reward the reader who makes it all the way through with some encouragement that she too can try similar policy development at home. We tell this story not only to entertain and amuse, there-fore, but to encourage other districts, states, and unions to give alterna-tive forms of teacher compensation a try, to convince them that it is not like eating glass—at least most of the time—and that many of the ob-stacles can be overcome by simply refusing to give up on an idea whose time has come. While some of the stars were aligned in Denver to make ProComp happen, there were many barriers, any one of which could have stopped ProComp in its tracks, barriers that other communities confront all the time. In parlance of the west, we would simply like to say that Denver folks just refused to let the sucker die.

As we have talked to others around the country and observed the media coverage of ProComp, we have discovered a few general miscon-ceptions about the salary system and how it was developed, false im-pressions that might discourage others from sticking first a toe, as they have recently done in California, and maybe later a foot into the waters of compensation reform. We would like to label some of these fallacies while linking to the storylines we developed earlier.

As much as we would have liked to present a top-ten list, we have found only eight important general misconceptions about ProComp. When we dispel them—some of which are outright wrong while others are simply not entirely accurate—we think the landscape for developing teacher PFP in other parts of the country starts to look a lot more fertile. We also highlight some of the lessons for entrepreneurial philanthropy that we think ProComp suggests. We then conclude with some specific lessons for making teacher PFP more widespread.

Common Misconceptions

The eight misconceptions we want to address include: (1) that Pro-Comp is the be-all and end-all of teacher compensation reform; (2) that the Denver Board of Education and the union enjoyed an unusual level of trust; (3) that members of the Denver Classroom Teachers Association were unified on the idea of PFP; (4) that DPS administration supported ProComp and pushed it on the union; (5) that PFP and Pro-Comp were central reforms for DPS and were essential as policy initiatives; (6) that conservative philanthropic organizations poured large amounts of money into ProComp; (7) that Colorado and Denver had the infrastructure and financing in place to ease ProComp along; and (8) that ProComp can be copied and imported by other districts without at least some of the processes that led to the compensation system's development.

The quotation that provides this chapter's subtitle comes from Jeff Buck, teacher member of the ProComp team and first ProComp member. Buck emphasizes that he does not mean teachers must "join Pro-Comp or die" or anything of that nature, rather, that urban school systems must change the way they do business, with reforms like ProComp essential to that change, or face serious consequences.

When Jeff Buck became the first to sign up for ProComp, he did take a metaphorical walk on the moon, likely advancing the PFP movement to a place it had never gone before. We would like to think that the U.S. Department of Education acknowledged as much when it distributed over 50 percent of the first round of the new TIF grant dollars to DPS in

November 2006. Further, other districts and states have explicitly modeled parts of their new teacher pay plans after ProComp. But even ProComp's strongest supporters recognize that its creation required compromise, that it has its strengths and limitations, that it is quite complex. ProComp perhaps moves teacher compensation halfway to a final goal. In school districts across the country, therefore, pragmatic unions partnering with boards of education and committed central office staffs have the opportunity to improve upon ProComp, learning from what Denver has done but understanding that they can do even better. In fact, part of the genius of the ProComp Agreement is that the union and the school district can make adjustments to ProComp itself, as they learn what works and what does not. We would be alarmed if "ProComp 2006" turns out to be the perfect plan for all time, partly because we would be shocked if Denver does not eventually improve its own system.

Second, we hope that chapters 2 through 5 dispel the myth that Denver enjoyed an unusual period of labor-management harmony during the PFP pilot and creation of ProComp. In fact, during most of the period of ProComp's development, the union and administration were fighting about something, distrustful of each other's motives, even doubting that ProComp would be approved ultimately, wary of committing too many resources to it. During the Denver effort, the union filed a lawsuit, refused to endorse a 2003 mill-levy tax increase advocated by the Board of Education, and annual negotiations over pay percentage increases for the existing salary system created tensions that at times appeared insurmountable. There was even talk of a strike. So a poor relationship between school labor and management is not a good excuse for failing to give compensation reform a try. The story of ProComp's development should also remind future reformers that the force of external accountability provided by civic leaders and philanthropy may help keep the union and the school district on track through difficult times.

Third, while DCTA often provided important leadership over the life of the PFP pilot and through ProComp's development, union membership remained deeply divided over not only the proposed alternative to the single salary schedule but the notion of whether the union should have agreed to a PFP pilot in the first place. In fact, just five weeks before the vote to adopt ProComp, internal polls showed that only 19 percent of teachers would vote in its favor. Further, during the campaign, union leadership did not tell teachers they should vote *for* the new system, staying neutral and telling members they should vote their consciences. Our narrative shows that DCTA clearly had some unique members and circumstances; however, we cannot attribute ProComp's success to the notion that Denver somehow had become a teacher union Shangri-la in which members of the association chanted the virtues of PFP in unison, religious in their devotion to ProComp.

Fourth, the assumption that the DPS administration and board were committed to the program and carefully building support for it could not be further from the truth. From the beginning of the PFP pilot through its early stages of implementation, DPS had so many other priorities that the effort existed within a skunk works to which few paid attention. While Jerry Wartgow provided more stability and a sense of forward direction, many high-level administrators continued to hold very mixed feelings about ProComp. Some did not think money motivated teachers; others appeared to believe that it was fruitless to invest too much energy in something the union would ultimately reject or in a project that would not advance student learning as much as other initiatives being undertaken by the school district. The idea that the union opposed ProComp and a forceful, unified administrative structure somehow propelled it forward is, well, preposterous.

Fifth, casual observers might believe that the development of ProComp took place in a very public way, as a central element of DPS's policy. This simply was not true. Chapter 3 reveals the PFP pilot's near invisibility to all but those working on the design team, in top management or in pilot schools. In fact, Phil Gonring, with the support of Rose's board and education committee, went to great lengths to keep the Board of Education and central staff's focus on PFP, even engineering a very public press conference with the governor to remind the Board of Education, the community, and the press that ProComp was still an important reform effort. We also suggest in chapter 3 that the lack of visibility actually might have helped—as the ProComp skunk works seemed to be effective because the process was marginalized, affording the design team and the JTF the luxuries of time and freedom to complete the pilot and think through the elements of a good compensation plan. Until the initiative went to Denver voters, ProComp was not generally held up as a signature element of DPS policies.

Sixth, given the fact that Colorado's Republican vanguard supported ProComp, some might conclude that conservative philanthropic groups wielded huge sums of money to buy the union's support and make ProComp work. They could bolster their argument by pointing to the fact that the Philanthropy Roundtable, conservative philanthropy's answer to the Council of Foundations, has featured ProComp on panels at two of its national education meetings. They might even rest their case by reminding us that Denver's Daniels Fund, considered one of Colorado's most conservative philanthropies, gave $1 million to the ProComp effort, while at the same time supporting vouchers, private schools, and the charter school movement.

But they would be wrong, for Rose Community Foundation and the Broad Foundation are philanthropies that no one would confuse as conservative foundations in the mold of Bradley, Walton, or Olin. Indeed, while Rose has paid for a conservative governor's health-policy analyst and a gun-law enforcement campaign, it also supports gay and lesbian causes, Planned Parenthood, and grassroots community organizing. While it has funded the development of a handful of charter schools, it is not religious in its commitment to school choice and remains neutral in the voucher debate but steadfast in its commitment to improving teacher quality. While the Broad Foundation may put pressure on the education establishment, it is clearly willing to work with labor, and it is public knowledge that Eli Broad himself is a big supporter of Democratic candidates. Indeed, ProComp did not result from some vast right-wing philanthropic conspiracy. In fact, plenty of conservatives have criticized ProComp for *not going far enough*, for its failure to tie the bulk of teacher pay to student achievement. On the other hand, liberals have challenged ProComp as just another effort that forces teachers to teach to the test. ProComp, alas, appears to make only pragmatists happy. So we would prefer to suggest that ProComp is the result of consortium of supporters from across the political spectrum in service of a pragmatic idea whose time had come.

Seventh, the larger context of education funding was hardly ideal for ProComp to thrive in Denver or in Colorado. One could argue that the low funding (Colorado is in the bottom quintile of the fifty states' K–12 per pupil spending, despite being in the top quintile of per capita income) created a bigger hurdle for ProComp, since it required more and new money. In addition, Colorado's Taxpayer Bill of Rights (TABOR), an addition to the state's constitution in 1992, mandates that all new taxes or tax increases go before the voters; local boards of education can not just bring in more revenue by allowing property tax assessment to grow with a flat mill-levy rate—all increases must go before the voters. TABOR, in fact, is the strictest fiscal constraint in the nation, and Pro-Comp would not exist if Denver voters had not explicitly agreed to raise their taxes to pay for it.

Finally, some school boards, superintendents, or even unions may want to copy the ProComp Agreement wholesale and hope to successfully introduce it into their districts. Perhaps a philanthropic organization will want to reproduce the agreement across the nation. We cannot imagine a more dangerous undertaking, as we believe it is necessary for teachers to help build and sustain a system that works for them, a lesson from the ProComp effort that should give school boards, governors, and other policy-makers pause before they try to dictate a system to teachers. As the board of education did in Denver, they may want to apply a little pressure to get the ball rolling, but it would be a mistake to foist something on a school system without a lot of internal discussion and debate. A central theme of chapters 2 through 5 is in fact that teacher and administrator creative intelligence flourishes if it is given the time and the resources to unfold. The result of that intelligence may in fact be good pay policy that works for one particular jurisdiction—but not necessarily another. While other jurisdictions can learn from ProComp (and that is part of the reason we are writing this book), we doubt that a brief, top-down introduction of PFP will work. Bill Slotnik agrees that community collaboration is critical and he worries a great deal about states trying to impose PFP upon districts from the top down.[1]

From initial discussion to actual implementation, ProComp took about eight years. It could easily have fallen apart at any one of several key junctures, as our narrative suggests. In fact, it developed because of the sustained entrepreneurial efforts of individuals operating both inside and outside of the policy community, not an instant decision made by policymakers.

Part of what sustained the long arc development of ProComp was philanthropic support, especially at critical junctures. We believe that ProComp's development can also inform the philanthropic world about achieving education reform. Philanthropy's role has recently been the topic of much critical attention, particularly around the national efforts of the Annenberg Foundation Challenge, the Broad Foundation Urban District Prize, and the Bill & Melinda Gates Foundation's Small School Initiative.[2] While even the largest philanthropic organizations have relatively minor resources compared to the $500 billion American K–12 education system, the sector does control the most flexible resources, which can be leveraged. The approximately $7 million total invested into ProComp by eight separate philanthropies will return more than a $250 million public investment over the next ten years of the program's implementation. Add to that the $22 million recently contributed to DPS by the TIF, a program that Slotnik believes would not have been approved by Congress without Denver's success, and we can see that philanthropies turned a relatively small investment into a huge financial return that we all hope will lead to better learning for Denver students.

Lessons for Philanthropy

When discussing the role foundations played in the success of ProComp, we risk overstating the importance of their willingness to influence the Board of Education's resolution to extend the length of the PFP pilot, the union's decision to adopt ProComp, and the public's vote to approve 3A. These expressions of will were important, but they obscure one of the most important lessons about philanthropy—in particular, how it can work with labor—that we have learned in writing this book.

Throughout the pilot, there were moments of both great collaboration and great tension between the union and philanthropies, Rose in particular. The tension reached its highest point during the campaign to promote the adoption of ProComp by DCTA. As we have already discussed, union leaders wished the foundations had not become involved, suggested that the campaign created division within and harmed the association. One teacher even went on the radio to say Rose was trying to destroy DCTA. This begs an important question, one we have recently asked DCTA's executive director, Bruce Dickinson: "Why is the union still willing to work with Rose on ProComp and other ventures?"

Dickinson's answer is interesting: "With the exception of a certain aspect of the ProComp campaign, we (the union) never felt that Rose had its thumb on us, that Rose was pulling strings during the pilot or the development of ProComp. Rose never told us what the compensation system should look like. We had complete control of that."[3]

His remarks remind us of former Colorado Education Association president Beverly Ausfahl's comments in chapter 5. It appears that Rose's and the other philanthropic partners' willingness to put their faith in a theory of learning and in teachers paid great dividends beyond the development of a new salary system. That the philanthropies committed themselves to support teacher learning and ideas engendered by that learning permitted them to more forcefully intervene in preserving the processes that allowed those ideas to flourish and ensuring they would be communicated effectively to the people who would ultimately make the decision to adopt ProComp.

From the beginning, it is fair to say, Rose betrayed a bias toward working with labor. The foundation did not believe it could push a magic button to make the union go away so it might work with the board of education to impose a new salary system unilaterally. Nor did it begrudgingly acknowledge the union's existence, find it abhorrent, and seek to bypass it. Rose adapted a pragmatic view, considering the union a key partner in compensation reform, even going so far to give it over $160,000 to mount a communication effort within schools. In so doing, it had no idea that it was strengthening a relationship that now could survive the turmoil of the ProComp campaign.

Besides reflecting on the relationship between teacher unions and philanthropy, we can also examine a successful relationship between a local philanthropy and a national one. From the perspective of local philanthropies, well-intentioned national foundations often come into communities with their own ideas, processes, and sets of assumptions that may or may not reflect on-the-ground realities or honor the intelligence of local communities. Sometimes, the foundations ask for matching dollars to support their projects and then three to five years later move on to new ideas and other towns, expecting the local communities to pick up the tab in the years that follow. The initial courtship can be seductive to local foundations, as program officers rush to tell their boards that they and a host of local philanthropies have turned a little bit of money, like magic beans, into a pot of gold. Those magic beans, however, grow into programs and, as in Denver, local philanthropies and governments continue to struggle to maintain projects national philanthropies abandoned years ago. We can speculate that the courtship is seductive to program officers in national foundations as well, as they go back to their boards and tell them that their ideas must have been good because several local foundations invested in them.

The Broad Foundation behaved very differently in Denver, taking advantage of the unique processes already proceeding within DPS and DCTA. While requiring a good degree of accountability, Broad allowed the design team to spend its money on what team members believed the project needed. Further, as discussed in chapters 4 and 5, it was the Broad Foundation's ability to plot strategy in real time, adapt to changing circumstances. and invest significant money quickly that helped secure ProComp's success.

As of late, analysts are spilling a lot of ink in their effort to explain why philanthropy has failed in its efforts to reform education. Too few, we believe, have explored the nature of the relationship between local communities and national philanthropies and how they both can do a better job of working together to improve outcomes for schools and students.

Finally, it is necessary to shine some light on the important role foundation boards play in setting the tone and parameters for what program officers do. Rose's founding president and chief executive officer, Don Kortz, and board of trustees made it clear that they expected program officers to be entrepreneurial, to behave like the CEOs of their own companies, to work on the margins and help make things happen in the community, subject to the normal oversight of a board of directors. Had they not given Gonring this latitude and support, he never would have asked for the first $1 million to support the PFP pilot, let alone the second. When the Rose board decided to make the grant, Gonring knew his trustees were investing in a powerful but commonsense idea whose time had come and that their decision was in part informed by their comfort with an entrepreneurial style of grant-making. Indeed, it is possible to argue that without Kortz's vision and a board of men and women who in fact had taken many risks of their own, Rose never would have taken a chance on PFP and ProComp may have never happened.

Lessons for Teacher-Compensation Reformers

The main lesson of this book is that it is possible for urban districts and unions to implement PFP and do it in a way that puts more salary in play than the meager 1 or 2 percent we see in PFP programs operating in other communities, salary that is usually on top of, not in place of, the single salary schedule. Successful policy entrepreneurship made ProComp viable, but our story is not one that highlights the importance or necessity of brilliance. Persistence, tenacity, inventiveness, and a capacity for improvisation propelled ProComp from vague notion to actual policy. As these traits are in abundant supply in school districts and unions across America, there should be few excuses for not giving PFP a go.

As we noted in chapter 1, the barriers to making PFP work are both political and technical. We believe that observers sometimes overestimate the political barriers (e.g., union opposition) and underestimate some of the technical issues (e.g., measuring performance). Both have to be resolved, and probably at the same time. Politically, it is clear that school board members and administrators will not place high priority on PFP unless they believe the unions will support it. The easiest way for DPS administrators to dismiss PFP and to put their resources elsewhere was to believe that, in the end, the union would vote ProComp down. They did not want to waste their time putting their eggs in the ProComp basket.

The fact that DCTA did vote in favor will hopefully change at least the perceptual landscape in other districts across the country. But districts also need help from the outside to make reforms like PFP work. We have shown how philanthropy provided essential financial and political support at crucial junctures and did not just sit back and watch. In Denver, the governor stepped up at one key point and the mayor was a huge supporter of ProComp. The voters signaled their approval in the strongest manner possible, by taxing themselves. Success required all of these actors' support.

In technical terms, PFP must be feasible and fair, not arbitrary, capricious, or developed with the intent of punishing bad teachers. Ideally, it should be designed to advance the goals of the school district and be as straightforward and simple as possible. An ultra-complicated pay structure will be incomprehensible and likely result in a lack of trust or huge burdens on central administration. ProComp, in fact, is on the border between just right and too complex; as a result, teachers were wary about how it would be implemented until it was explained to them adequately.

Another technical issue that must be resolved is whether alternative teacher pay should be tied to group or individual achievement. While ProComp focuses on the results produced by individual teachers, other districts have emphasized team goals and rewards to groups of teachers or even entire school communities, including custodians and other support staff. ProComp includes such a component; however, the reward is only a small part of the entire ProComp package and is reserved for teachers only.

We worry that the team or school approach may be too broad and imprecise to achieve the goal of higher student achievement. A key finding from the PFP pilot was that individual incentives do not cause destructive competition among teachers. We believe it is cynical to suggest that teachers cannot be judged on the results they produce in classrooms on their own. If they cannot be, why would we not just throw a bunch of high school graduates into classrooms and expect them to produce similar results? Most teachers know they perform better than the average high school graduate would and get up and go to work every day knowing they are going to make a difference in the lives of their students. Most of them do. Why not treat them as the professionals they are and pay them for the results they produce, especially because we learned that compensation geared toward individual achievement does not sabotage collegiality?

It is understandable that teachers are concerned that we do not have the systems and technology in place to measure their performance in a fair way, especially when state accountability systems, like the one in Colorado, do not always distinguish between schools serving high need populations and those enrolling only middle- and upper-class kids. Teachers need to be convinced that there are value-added measures that give them a chance to demonstrate their effectiveness. As diagnostic tests and human resource management systems that track students and teachers get better, the science of measuring student learning and associating it with specific teachers is improving. In fact, Denver's system uses a value-added model of measuring student performance to make compensation decisions. In the broad scope of time, these are relatively recent innovations that teachers and parents are just getting used to. Soon, hopefully, as the research techniques improve, teachers will come to understand that connecting student learning to individual teachers makes a lot of sense.

Someday we imagine the unions will figure out that they can turn the accountability movement on its head and make it work for them, making it a way to increase wages for members. School districts may even compete over teachers, offering signing bonuses and increased wages to individuals who have produced results in other districts. They may even understand the need for compensation systems geared toward the new generation of teachers who want to distinguish themselves instead of being paid the same wages as those who produce inferior results.

Before we appear Pollyannaish, however, we have to offer an important disclaimer, reminding those who would suggest that all compensation should be tied to test scores that in Denver the results of the state test can be traced back to approximately 35 percent of the district's teachers, as we discussed in chapter 1. Nevertheless, as Denver proved, it is possible to build into a salary system a component that takes into account the state test and grants significant salary increases (3% each year) to teachers whose students outperform expectations based on previous assessments of learning. In Denver, both teachers and administrators decided that as long as the government is going to tie high stakes to state testing then it makes sense for school districts to offer increased compensation to those who teach in high-stakes positions and produce results. In short, ProComp is an example of a union making the law work for its teachers. To advance beyond what Denver has accomplished in terms of linking pay to student growth, school districts will have to develop or find fair and statistically valid measurements that can be used to make compensation decisions for teachers in academic disciplines not tested by the states. They will also need to figure out how to pay for those assessments.

The fact that state tests affect so few teachers helps resolve another technical issue, namely that compensation systems should likely employ multiple measures, not just one. Just as some students may feel that a mixed grading approach is fair if it incorporates multiple-choice questions, short answers, and longer essays, teachers may find a mixed approach fairer as well. These approaches acknowledge the complex task that is teaching and allows the district to tie its pay system to its broader goals, such as retaining teachers in hard-to-staff schools, acknowledging and rewarding student achievement, and providing an incentive for teachers to help their students develop necessary knowledge and skills.

ProComp uses four different forms of differential compensation, most of which have a few subcomponents. For instance, teachers who do not teach a class that is assessed by the state test can still get into the student-learning game by achieving student growth objectives. There is, however, no silver bullet in Denver that other jurisdictions should feel compelled to fire. High-income districts, for instance, may not need market incentives: there is incentive enough in teaching affluent kids. But high-income districts may want to reward student achievement and the demonstration of knowledge and skill.

The technical decisions also shape and, in some cases, ease the political barriers. By not forcing all currently employed teachers to opt into ProComp at the start, Denver avoided creating strong opposition from teachers who would never want to be part of ProComp. Incorporating all new hires into the system builds support over time. A mix of reward mechanisms provides different teachers with different foci upon which to devote their own professional attention, which would be blunted by a single reward structure, especially if it had been tied entirely to one output, student achievement. Further, rather than developing a system aimed at punishing "bad teachers," Denver developed a plan that focused on the upside, giving all teachers the opportunity to build career earnings by producing results.

But we would like to conclude this chapter with a discussion of a final technical issue because this issue has become political as well. Should PFP systems require new and additional streams of revenue, or should they be supported by the simple redistribution of funds already in existence? While some propose teacher salaries are low compared to those of similarly educated professionals, others argue for a more nuanced view, suggesting that the actual hourly wage is competitive with that of other professions, pointing to the summers teachers have off and a defined workday that may not stretch to eight hours. We know, however, as parents and, in some of our cases, as former K–12 teachers that many teachers endeavor to be very good at their craft; between writing lesson plans, grading papers until midnight, reading texts, calling and meeting parents, handling extracurricular activities, and creating materials, they work a lot of 12-hour days, sometimes on the weekends and in the summer too.

We understand, because we have seen them as well, that some teachers do not share the same work ethic: the $50,000 a year gym teacher who rolls out the balls and sits on the bleachers five periods a day; the English teacher who lectures out of a grammar book all day long, sells real estate during her planning period, and is out the door to show houses at 3:00 p.m.; the social studies teacher who assigns word finds, crossword puzzles, and research papers (but never teaches his students how to write one); the history teacher whose lectures on contemporary American history end in 1976 because that is the first year he taught; and the fifth grade teacher who believes that quality writing does not extend beyond good penmanship.

But boards of education and governors cannot legislate compensation policy with these teachers in mind. The impulse to differentiate pay cannot come from the belief that teachers are lazy, bad, or incompetent. In rethinking teacher pay, policymakers have to imagine the person they want teaching kids in their community, such as the recent graduate of a top-tier university, a young man or woman who is full of passion, talent, energy, and potential. Imagine that person signing her first contract at age 23 for $32,000 a year, with no other dream but to teach English in a challenging urban high school. Each day she teaches 150 students, many of whom are reading and writing at fifth- and sixth-grade levels and have social and emotional issues or learning disabilities. But she loves teaching novels to her third-period class of tenth graders because many of the fictional characters resonate with her students. She even looks forward to an eighth-period class with a handful of gang members and youth acquainted with the justice system, many of whom are in school only because it is a condition of their probation. Imagine the creativity required to teach them *Beowulf*, which the district curriculum demands all eleventh graders read. She relishes the challenge.

Undaunted by the challenges, she establishes a sentence-writing club for some of her tenth graders who still cannot write one and meets with them twice a week at 6:30 a.m. She coaches the girls' softball team and chaperones dances where she breaks up fights that even the police will not interrupt. She wants to be very good at what she does and takes state and federal mandates very seriously, believing passionately that she can get her sixth-grade readers up to the tenth-grade level by the time the state assessment is administered. A few months later, though, she receives student results below those she'd hoped for. Although many of her students showed significant growth, it is not enough. She wonders why all her hard work did not pay off, thinks about what she could do to improve her practice, but worries that she may not be cut out for teaching after all. She asks, "Is this worth the $32,000 I'm now making, the $33,200 I'll make in a year, the $40,000 I'll earn if I somehow have time to complete the masters I'm working on?" She knows she is talented enough to consider other professions, too, but instead contemplates moving to a suburban district where the work will be easier and she will have more time for friends, family, and the completion of her masters.

As we think of technical solutions to advance PFP, this is the person who should inspire us as we imagine better compensation policy. This is the person to whom we might want to pay $60,000 and even $70,000 far earlier in her career than the single salary schedule allows, so that she too can enjoy a middle-class lifestyle that may include a sip or two of a fancy umbrella drink in at least a three-star resort. This is also the person we want to inspire teachers already employed in school districts to become, as we use financial incentives to encourage their development. We hope our teacher in this example, like many entering teaching today, would relish the idea of tying money to results. And this is the trade-off the Denver teachers explicitly made—more money for more accountability.

As other communities contemplate changing teacher pay, and the technical and political issues that accompany that change, inevitably some in the chattering classes will complain that teachers are already adequately compensated and that better systems can be devised simply by reorganizing the money already available. We have our doubts about this. While there were political reasons to increase the pool of funds available to compensate Denver teachers by $25 million, there were also pragmatic ones. ProComp leaders understood that if they were to meet one of their goals—to attract and retain high-quality teachers— they were going to have to pay teachers more than they would receive in other districts, and they were going to have to give talented individuals the opportunity to build salary at much faster rates than the traditional single salary schedule allows. We would encourage other jurisdictions to consider the same. Unfortunately, many school districts in our own

Denver metropolitan area do not by law have the capacity to increase their property-tax rates in any substantial way to seriously raise salaries. Our suspicion is that school districts across the country will confront a similar issue.

Where is the money going to come from, then? This is not a question we can answer easily, but we do not think we should just throw our hands in the air and surrender to those who say we should never raise our taxes. Certainly, the people in Denver did not give in to that impulse and increased their taxes substantially. We are optimists and believe that local communities, potentially states, and maybe even the federal government will come to the same conclusion. While unions should not expect more money for teachers without connecting those dollars to results, policymakers should not expect a world-class education system without teachers who can deliver it. Perhaps once the unions are willing to do some horse-trading, we will get more traction out of our government leaders. This is a negotiation we would like to see take place—even if it is, alas, over a bargaining table.

8

Perspectives on Educational Entrepreneurship

We Took Whatever Washed Up on the Shore

We have told the tale of the development of ProComp in Denver, paying particular attention to the specific strategies and actions of key leaders. From the narrative, we extrapolated lessons about philanthropy and teacher compensation reform, and reflected on some possible misconceptions about ProComp. In this final chapter, we put ProComp into the context of theoretical approaches to policy development and, in so doing, provide some lessons for the emerging literature on entrepreneurialism as expressed in education reform.

The American political system is set up explicitly to encourage slow change at all levels, with multiple veto points, three branches of government, and various vocal constituencies often arguing for the status quo. It is always somewhat surprising when an important and dynamic new public-policy idea actually gets approved and put into action. The surprise packs an even greater punch when the idea had been blocked frequently in other jurisdictions because it was considered impossible to implement or simply untenable.

Surprised when Denver teachers and then taxpayers voted to approve and fund ProComp, skeptical school reformers asked, "How did Denver do that?" We have devoted this book to answering that question, in part because ProComp may be one of the critical first steps in a much more widespread national movement toward paying public school teachers differently. But, when, why, where, and how new policies come into being are important questions in all realms of public policy. And they are particularly interesting and important questions in education policy, where, despite lots of churning and ongoing discussions about reform, real fundamental change to basic systems is not common.[1] This is true in part because many powerful interests, sometimes collectively referred to as the "education establishment," express a wariness of quick and radical change and cling to a desire to maintain business as usual. Analysts are quick to identify teacher unions as the stiffest bulwark against meaningful progress; however, administrators, school boards, and even parents often veto the evolution of the American education system, as if they were the Kansas State Board of Education trying to prevent Charles Darwin from sneaking into the state through Nebraska.

We will argue that policy entrepreneurship enabled Denver to break through the bulwark. To conclude that argument successfully, however, before turning to entrepreneurialism, the framework that works best, we first must examine briefly a few other contending theoretical explanations for how ProComp might have emerged. We then examine broader notions of policy entrepreneurship, to place the efforts around ProComp into context and to show the connections between what the theories of entrepreneurship tell us and what we have demonstrated in previous chapters to have happened in Denver.

Explanations of Policy Change

There are three main explanatory frameworks for policy change. The first emphasizes the fairly stable relationship of multiple political actors who form opposing coalitions but maintain some ability to learn and to refine their positions to address changes in the real world. This is most well developed in Sabatier's Advocacy Coalition Framework, or ACF, which was created so policymakers better understand the relative inertia of competing coalitions on many key issues, but also to allow for the possibility of gradual or incremental learning and change.[2] For example, shifts in policy views on the relative advantages of nuclear power generation are explained well by the ACF, as nuclear power moved from widely popular, after WWII, to very unpopular, after Three Mile Island and other generator site and cost problems, to a more balanced position today, where some environmental advocates view nuclear power more positively than carbon-generating power alternatives.

The development of ProComp, however, does not seem to fit this framework well. There was never a strong stable coalition pushing for PFP; indeed, as we showed, DPS administration often had little interest in this reform moving forward, so it had to exist inside a skunk works buried deep within Denver Public Schools. And just five weeks before the union vote on whether to adopt the new salary system, only a handful of teachers revealed, through polling, that they would actually support it. In short, five years into Denver's PFP initiative, ProComp appeared to have almost no constituency.

The second major explanatory framework also takes a long-term perspective on policy change but borrows effectively from evolutionary theories in the physical sciences. Baumgartner and Jones developed a punctuated equilibrium framework that tries to assess why policy directions seem to be static, or at most incremental, at most points in time, but then a sudden eruption of change can take place, often surprising observers and sometimes even participants themselves.[3] The scholars draw an analogy to punctuated equilibrium models in evolutionary biology, which have gone beyond Darwin's initial ideas of gradualism to demonstrate that evolutionary changes can sometimes come at a remarkable pace, even in the continuing and overarching context of more customary long, slow change. Baumgartner and Jones use national policy agenda data, and sometimes budgetary analyses, to show how underlying dynamics can be shifting, even when the surface level appears to show inertia, followed by an abrupt policy change. A good example is environmental policy, where a gradual, subsurface focus of attention emerged in the 1950s and 1960s, followed by remarkably quick policy changes in the late 1960s, with the rapid establishment of the Clean Air and Clean Water Acts and the Environmental Protection Agency. It is perhaps possible that Denver's ProComp is a leading sign of an abrupt national shift toward PFP, but until the shift happens we will reserve judgment on the overall application of the punctuated-equilibrium systems model.

An astute observer might be able to integrate each of these perspectives and lenses on ProComp's development. Though, as we demonstrated, a few seeds were planted earlier than most observers realize during labor-management negotiations in the 1980s and early 1990s, ProComp did not have a decades-long history in Denver of different groups or coalitions providing support or opposition, and gradually, or even abruptly, changing their views. While it may be the indicator of a future of national change on this issue, the policy punctuation in Denver was one actively sought by a small number of people, rather than a surface reflection that captured shifting underlying dynamics.

ProComp and teacher PFP in Denver was a vague idea at first, proposed as a side issue during thorny labor-negotiation issues about annual percentage salary increases. As time went on, what would become ProComp was supported very tentatively by a few individuals in key positions, especially by a few members of the Board of Education, but each of them probably held a different view of what it might become and how they might use it to advance their other policy agendas.

A third explanatory framework thus holds more promise and points us in the direction of focusing upon entrepreneurs. The multiple-streams framework advanced by John Kingdon suggests that policy solutions, problems, and politics are all part of a complicated society, streaming along at any given point in time. When conditions are ripe for a policy window to open up, a savvy entrepreneur can couple a solution with a problem that has arisen on the political agenda.[4] The timing of this coupling can sometimes be systematically exploited by policy entrepreneurs, though at other times any coupling is really quite random and not highly predictable; indeed, in an extreme version of the multiple-stream approaches, the garbage-can model, the linking is almost completely random. Still, ProComp was surely not a random accident. We believe that the intentional coupling of multiple streams by key entrepreneurs is the best framework within which to examine ProComp's development; it puts a central focus on policy entrepreneurship.

Entrepreneurship is a complicated subject of study. Entrepreneurs were first examined carefully in business studies, where they are assessed as the key people who create new products, new firms, or even new markets, and often gain large financial rewards as a consequence. Compared to most economics and business studies, where precise quantitative modeling is the favored approach, entrepreneurship is a much more fuzzy arena, filled with generalizations and theories focused on personal characteristics and traits.

This lack of precision is even more pronounced when the concept of entrepreneurship is examined within the public sector. Policy scholars have long talked about key policy entrepreneurs who advance legislation or ideas, but only recently have they attempted to focus on some key features or elements. A larger literature has also grown, using the related terms "public" and "social" entrepreneurship.

Following Kingdon, who identified entrepreneurs as a systematic force for change in a chaotic environment, other researchers have tried to increase the precision of identifying policy entrepreneurs. Mark Schneider and Paul Teske focused on the role of policy entrepreneurs in local governments, highlighting their central role in policy change but also trying to understand their motivations, the obstacles they face, and the tools they utilize to achieve and sustain policy change.[5] We will apply this focus to the development of ProComp.

Policy Entrepreneurship and Education

Fortunately, we can develop this entrepreneurial framework with direct input from two key ProComp entrepreneurs—coauthors Phil Gonring and Brad Jupp. This allows us to test ideas that Teske and other academics have developed in the more theoretical world, against the realities of personalities, pressures, and the world of education, and see what works best as explanation.

Policy entrepreneurs in education are generally seen as people who are trying to change the school system in some significant and fundamental way, perhaps even disrupting or transforming it. This may come from outside the system, as with those who support and advance vouchers, charter schools, or even private firms providing tutoring or test preparation that may have grander aspirations. Or the entrepreneurial push may come from actors within. Indeed, the broader literature on entrepreneurship, mostly from the business context, added a new term—"intrapreneurship"—to recognize that entrepreneurs are not only individuals with ideas who start small, new firms that sometimes grow into large, successful ones but also those who might transform a large existing organization from within. In our story, we have an education establishment intrapreneur in Jupp, who pushed for Pro-Comp within his union, and an outside entrepreneur in Gonring, who used his access to philanthropic resources to encourage change from outside the system.

Whether from within or without, those seeking to make major changes in education policy must have an entrepreneurial mindset if they hope to create disruptive or fundamentally transformative changes by taking a risk and seizing opportunities to provide new services or existing services in new ways. These entrepreneurs no doubt seek some individual rewards, though usually not the financial profits that are the typical assumed reward for business entrepreneurs, but their activities can facilitate what Schumpeter called "creative destruction" in the larger system.[6]

The focus on entrepreneurial mindset presumes that we can identify common personality characteristics in entrepreneurs. Early research in the 1950s and 1960s suggested that entrepreneurs were at the extreme end of risk-takers, and that their basic personality traits include a strong need for achievement, a high internal locus of control, a sense of urgency, and a desire to change the status quo, some of which appears prominently in the development of ProComp, as we illustrate especially in chapters 4 and 5.[7] More recent research suggests more variation, however, and has called into question whether we can develop a comprehensive list of essential personality traits or characteristics of entrepreneurs.[8] This research argues that entrepreneurs are likely to be rated highly on their salesmanship ability more often than their risk-seeking behavior, and they are less likely than most others to care about what other people think about them. Both Gonring and Jupp were good, thick-skinned salespeople for PFP, but also people with a sense of urgency about improving urban education.

This raises the question of why entrepreneurial types would be attracted to education policy. Scholars have noted that within the public education system, "there is little reward for taking entrepreneurial risks and succeeding, while there are significant personal and professional costs associated with taking such risks and failing."[9] The American public education system, like most of our public institutions, includes elements of democracy, bureaucracy, and citizen participation that provide numerous checks, balances, and veto points, all of which greatly increase the challenges for potential education entrepreneurs. Standard career paths for teachers and administrators, union contracts, informal norms within school systems, parental satisfaction with the current system, and the high visibility of any public decisions involving children all tend to favor inertia over change. For teachers, administrators, and staff, good and safe careers can be built by staying well within the boundaries of standard practice.

ProComp and Entrepreneurship

But policy entrepreneurs do emerge in education and they generally need to accomplish three basic sets of tasks. They must: (1) respond to opportunities, (2) take risks to fill gaps, and (3) build organizations and networks with other people. Key ProComp actors did in fact perform these tasks as the new salary system moved from idea to policy.

Every important policy change starts somewhere. In this case, several important actors in Denver gradually became alert to the opportunities that annual teacher pay negotiations raised in the Denver Public Schools. Viewed from a national perspective, however, Denver did not face a particular crisis of teacher pay or qualifications in the late 1990s—like many struggling urban districts, there were constant calls for improvement and reform, but these were not at a magnitude higher than in most other American cities.

The idea of introducing PFP into the annual teacher contract negotiations was discussed well before anyone on any side took it very seriously. Both Jupp and Gonring, coming from very different places, were slow to see how PFP could affect real reform for urban school districts and teachers.

It was quite unusual for teachers union leaders like Jupp, and Bruce Dickinson and Andrea Giunta at the time, to be alert to the opportunity presented by PFP, about which most of the DCTA membership was highly skeptical, and especially to jump then into the risky business of actually trying to transform the policy idea into practice. This required a thick skin and a sense of perceiving the potential for success where most others predicted sure failure. In citing Jupp as their "innovator of the year," the Progressive Policy Institute wrote: "what really makes Brad an innovator is that he's a die hard union member and was the Denver Classroom Teachers Association point person on the district-union team that designed and sold Pro-Comp to the city's teachers. . . . Pro-Comp doesn't go as far as some would like, and much farther than others want, but it would not have gone anywhere without a visionary like Brad Jupp to help lead the effort."[10]

At the same time, Gonring's board had given him permission to think in a risky, entrepreneurial manner, rather than playing it safe with less controversial, more comfortable grants to school districts. Even the largest national philanthropic players in education policy, like the huge Annenberg and Bill & Melinda Gates Foundations, have relatively small resources compared to the more than $500 billion American public education system. If they really want to leverage significant change, supporting moderate and less risky reforms seems unlikely to achieve that goal; this is particularly true for a smaller, local foundation.[11]

What would become ProComp emerged from a 1999 agreement between the union and school board to develop a PFP pilot program that would unfold over four years. With few or no national examples of how to do it right, the construction of the initial agreement presented significant problems that would make it difficult for the pilot to produce positive results. Moreover, the union and the school district did not have time to build the pilot on a stable political foundation, so the Denver project appeared poised to join the list of failed attempts at PFP.

This scenario raised a number of risks for the entrepreneurial actors who wanted to move this process forward. Gonring, Jupp, and others had to utilize their salesmanship, networking, and organization-building skills to make rapid progress. They quickly discovered that this was not easy. As the pilot began, however, everything slowed down. Changing leadership, among other factors, created challenges. Five DPS superintendents held power in the district over a critical three-year period of the pilot, which is unusually fast turnover, even in the difficult, highly politicized context of American urban school districts. Churning leadership made it very difficult to develop and sustain any single direction in policy and practice; it also created huge problems with personnel continuity, trust, and relationship-building. In addition, Denver's mandated annual collective-bargaining negotiations routinely pushed the pilot to the bottom of school-district priorities. During this time, the Board of Education continued to put much of its own focus on improving the entry-level pay of teachers, independent of performance, and focused on many issues besides teacher compensation.

Perhaps surprisingly, ProComp leaders often found working with the school district more difficult than working with the union. In fact, many central-office administrators were just as hostile to pay for performance as some teachers, an antagonism that reveals the Catch-22 embedded in the story of ProComp's development: key administrators really did not want to put the necessary work into creating the systems to support early ProComp efforts, since they either did not believe the union would ever vote to adopt the new system or thought there were other, more important priorities. Countless delays in the development of important supporting programs and materials ensued as a result.

But entrepreneurship also requires persistence. And Gonring, Jupp, and others were nothing if not persistent. They were able to patch together the right networks and organizations at the right time to propel the project forward—the design team, the skunk works, the Joint Task Force, coalitions of foundations and political heavyweights, and two political campaigns. In reality, policy entrepreneurs do not know what obstacles they may confront. They need flexibility, persistence, and a willingness to use the tools at their disposal to advance their cause.

Entrepreneurial Strategies

In performing the tasks we enumerate above, successful policy entrepreneurs often employ a common set of strategies. In his book *The Art of Political Manipulation* Riker even coined a new term—"heresthetics"—for the set of strategies he saw employed by successful policy entrepreneurs, who set about structuring their political world to ensure victory (the term itself comes from Greek roots meaning "choosing and electing").[12] At the risk of selling short their professional development programs, we doubt whether the NEA or the Council of Foundations provide heresthetic training for union leaders and program officers; however some of the elements of heresthetics nonetheless reveal themselves in the actions of key ProComp actors.

One key element of heresthetics is the ability to add a new dimension to an otherwise gridlocked debate. By doing so, entrepreneurs can reframe the problem and also make some headway toward solving the central dilemma. While this was not done explicitly by Jupp or Gonring, in retrospect, it appears to explain well what happened in the earliest emergence of the idea of ProComp. In politics, two groups are often engaged in difficult and unproductive negotiations on a single key issue, across a single policy dimension, such as the percentage of increase in teacher salaries. A savvy entrepreneur might introduce a new dimension to the discussion, one that alters the perceptions of the two parties about the central issue. Essentially, ProComp did this by changing the continual, annual teacher salary negotiations from a fight over, say, 2 percent versus 3 percent raises for all teachers to a completely new way of thinking about teacher compensation, where some teachers might get much larger raises while others receive little or nothing.

Thus, in retrospect, we are not surprised that the idea of PFP arose in Denver during those periods of salary negotiations when progress appeared to be completely blocked. Thoughtful participants were looking for a better way to handle this problem. Jupp, in particular, came to a critical inflection point in his thinking about PFP after a bloody and contentious contract negotiation and three-day strike in 1994, a work action that yielded only a 0.2 percent pay increase for the teachers union members. Both DCTA and the DPS negotiators seemed to recognize that they were fighting over crumbs of a smaller pie each year and that adding a new dimension to teacher pay might produce a win for both labor and management. However, in a risk-averse environment, no one was willing to actually push for the changes that would create that new dimension. Finally, in the late 1990s, school board member Laura Lefkowitz pushed. By then, fortunately, reformers like Jupp demonstrated a willingness to advance the ball despite the defensive positions around them, yielding the surprise that PFP in Denver did not die the quick death that it often suffers in other school districts.

Another strategic tool is the use of rhetoric—that is, actually using good and persuasive arguments to try to change participants' minds about key issues. Often in politics and policy, we do not necessarily believe that the minds of other actors can really be changed, and yet, at some level, this is required for any important policy change to occur. Clearly, Jupp, Gonring, and others made important rhetorical efforts, especially before the teachers union actually voted to accept ProComp, as we discuss in chapter 4, when minds needed to be changed with evidence or the whole enterprise would have met the unsuccessful fate of most prior PFP proposals. There were numerous other occasions, within the union, within the JTF, in philanthropic discussions and other arenas, in which Gonring and Jupp used rhetorical arguments to push the process forward successfully.

Another tool often employed by entrepreneurs is "arbitrage," the borrowing of an idea from one sector and adopting it in another. Interestingly, while it might have appeared from the outside that ProComp advocates were using a form of arbitrage, by suggesting that PFP could be transferred from the private to the public sector, Jupp and Gonring themselves almost never consciously used it. They understood that the compensation practices of business (or even those of higher education) are not easily translatable to public K–12 education and that simple ar bitrage analogies are naive at best. The analogy to compensation models in the private sector did provide some resonance for outside actors, however—especially businesspeople who supported the PFP notion, including members of key boards. It fit their own conceptions of successful policy arbitrage and common sense. Jupp and Gonring tactically used analogies to private-sector compensation systems to their advantage when it was necessary to help move ProComp forward. Businessmen like Bruce Benson made the business-ProComp connection more publicly only late in the game, as ProComp headed for the public vote. Business analogies, frankly, tend to drive teachers away from the bargaining table, so future reformers should use arbitrage at their own peril and only with the right audiences.

Despite our elucidation of entrepreneurial tasks and strategies in the paragraphs above, neither Jupp nor Gonring report having a particular metacognitive moment during the development of ProComp when they thought, "Hey, I am an entrepreneur leading national policy change." Nor did they ever think of their actions as occurring within the context of a theory of entrepreneurialism or that the tasks they performed or the strategies they employed had names—especially ones they may not have been able to pronounce. Jupp simply believed that Denver could see an open policy window when most other districts could not and had an opportunity to do something different about compensation. Jupp thinks that, rather than as entrepreneurs on a cutting edge, all of the key players in ProComp saw themselves as pragmatic problem-solvers who were fortunate to be working in an environment that had been opened to entrepreneurial possibilities, with the expectation that success was possible.

Gonring kept focused on his faith that the process would yield one of the most progressive teacher-compensation systems in the country and therefore offer far better opportunities for teachers and children in DPS. He would not have articulated a theoretical framework for his actions and was simply determined to employ any strategy within reason to give the project the greatest chance to succeed. The entrepreneurial style of Rose Community Foundation provided a context and a support system for realizing that commitment to social progress.

Other analysts have made advances in our understanding of entrepreneurs in the education sector, especially those writing in a recent book-length study of educational entrepreneurialism. In one chapter of that volume, Williams characterizes types of education entrepreneurs who emerge within school districts in colorful terms, highlighting "James Deans [rebels with a cause], Johnny Appleseeds [explicitly spreading ideas], Destiny Grabbers [linking to national reforms], and Bulls Managing the China Shop [breaking things]," among other types.[13] While one could find elements of what Gonring and Jupp did in most of these characters, no one of these descriptions fits terribly well. A more apt nickname, given what we have learned, is "John Coltranes," a term we coin to describe those who exhibit improvisational entrepreneurialism, but without the influence of heroin, and while hitting far more wrong notes in one day than left Coltrane's saxophone in a lifetime.

The evolution of ProComp suggests that in addition to using the tools of their trade, educational entrepreneurs must be able to improvise, working with different ensembles when necessary, taking surprises as they come, rethinking any given approach, taking another approach until yet other surprises or opportunities render that approach unworkable, insufficient, or invalid. In reality, policy entrepreneurs do not know what types of obstacles they may confront. They need flexibility, persistence, and a willingness to use the tools at their disposal—in other words, an ability to invent on the fly.

Armed with a powerful idea, but with a seemingly more powerful set of barriers lined up against them, ProComp leaders had to make use of anything worthwhile that washed up on the shore. As we've shown, Jupp, Gonring, and others found various means to the final end. Such improvisational entrepreneurship actually fits the Kingdon multiple-streams model fairly well, though Kingdon's approach tends to imply a onetime entrepreneurial coupling process. ProComp entrepreneurs coupled whatever was useful from their respective environments with the idea of PFP to move it forward, but they did this multiple times. They jettisoned less useful concepts or ideas when necessary as they employed tactics and strategies that presented themselves only as the project unfolded.

ProComp's development does not follow the detailed script of a calculated business plan. It is, instead, a story of people with entrepreneurial inclinations and a willingness to learn and change course. None of them had a specific initial vision of what Denver's compensation system should look like. They used what made sense, discarded what did not, recalibrated, took a breath, then recalibrated again.

Sources of Entrepreneurial Energy

As we hope we have illustrated in some depth, while our focus is mainly on the actions of the two central entrepreneurs and coauthors here, their efforts would have amounted to nothing without the actions of other players in the drama that produced ProComp. Many others clearly injected entrepreneurial energy into the project at crucial times, even if they were not involved every step of the way.

This tension is part of a larger debate in the field of entrepreneurship studies about whether there are just a small number of truly amazing entrepreneurs, most of whom we identify in retrospect by their great successes (the few), or whether there are many entrepreneurs acting within our economic and political systems all the time (the many). Some of the many succeed, but most fail, so no one focuses much attention on their efforts or even knows that they have tried.

We believe that it took both the few and the many to make ProComp happen. DPS superintendent Irv Moskowitz and board member Laura Lefkowitz saw the early potential for PFP. Together they pushed the idea forward at a crucial juncture when no one else was yet championing it. Later, board leaders Les Woodward and Elaine Berman believed strongly that ProComp could and should work. They helped stabilize DPS during two leadership transitions, hired Jerry Wartgow with ProComp as a clear priority, supported the pilot at key junctures, and worked tirelessly on the 3A campaign. While Wartgow may not have always believed teachers would embrace ProComp, he engineered the skunk works, campaigned for Broad Foundation support, and hired key staff members—in particular Andre Pettigrew and Rich Allen, who would ensure that PFP plans would run smoothly in their departments. To wide applause from ProComp supporters, Wartgow also settled the board's contract dispute with the union at a time when the 3A mill-levy campaign could have been scuttled.

On the union and teacher side, while many of the key players maintained a neutral position on whether teachers should adopt ProComp, they did not wreck the reform's chances when they had the opportunity to do so. Dickinson laid the groundwork for a successful pilot through his work with TURN and his willingness to discuss with DCTA membership as early as 1998 the possibility of altering the single salary schedule. He was instrumental in negotiating 1999's labor agreement that allowed the pilot to proceed and engineered an effort to communicate to members the details of the pilot and the new compensation system. As president of DCTA during the teacher vote to adopt ProComp, Becky Wissink helped shepherd the PFP pilot during her two years on the design team, weathered the storms created by her el Niño of a decision to allow DCTA to consider what no other teachers union in America would. And teacher members of the JTF made critical contributions to ProComp's design, rendering it workable, fair, and likely the most progressive teacher pay system in the United States. Connie White, Shirley Scott, Henry Roman, Jeff Buck, and others continue to oversee the creation and revision of key elements of ProComp as the salary system enters the transition period.

Bill Slotnik of CTAC provided critical assistance to the design team as it worked to get the pilot up and running, pushed the school district and union harder than they thought they could be pushed, and, most importantly, strove to ensure that the school district perceived the transformation of a compensation system as a whole-district reform effort, not an isolated teacher-pay experiment. And his organization's comprehensive research study enabled union leadership and district administrators to move forward with a system that set the single salary schedule on its head.

These were key players among the many others whose entrepreneurial efforts fueled ProComp's success. But their sometimes isolated efforts probably would also have gone for naught without more sustained entrepreneurial pushes. It is clear to Teske that these pushes came from within the system, from a teacher who in 1994 had thought that PFP was an inappropriate way to pay teachers (Jupp) and from outside the system by a former teacher and school leader (Gonring) who was backed by the board of an organization committed to taking risks. These two players, whose friendship was not incidental to the joint efforts they made on behalf of ProComp, propelled the process with a combination of skill, luck, and determination that is apparent.

Though difficult to achieve, the entrepreneurial process that produced ProComp should engender some optimism that American urban education can be reformed, and not only by forces that would entirely replace the current system. What matters most is simple persistence and a willingness to improvise—even if you hit a few wrong notes along the way.

Notes

Chapter 1

1. See Ronald Johnson and Gary Libecap, *The Federal Civil Service System and the Problem of Bureaucracy: The Economics and Politics of Institutional Change* (Chicago: University of Chicago Press, 1994), for a discussion of civil service reform and development from an economic perspective.
2. James Q. Wilson, *Bureaucracy: What Government Does and Why* (New York: Basic Books, 1989).
3. David Osborne and Ted Gaebler, *Reinventing Government: How the Entrepreneurial Spirit Is Transforming the Public Sector* (New York: Plume, 1992).
4. See, for example, Gary Miller, *Managerial Dilemmas: The Political Economy of Hierarchy* (Cambridge: Cambridge University Press, 1992).
5. See, for example, Dale Ballou, "Pay for Performance in Public and Private Schools," *Economics of Education Review* 20 (2001): 51–61; Thomas Dee and Benjamin Keys. "Does Merit Pay Reward Good Teachers? Evidence from a Randomized Experiment," *Journal of Policy Analysis and Management* 23 (2004): 471–88; Carolyn Kelley, "Implementing Teacher Compensation Reform in Public Schools: Lessons from the Field." *The Journal of School Business Management* 8 (1996): 37–54; Richard Murnane and David Cohen. "Merit Pay and the Evaluation Problem: Why Most Merit Pay Plans Fail and a Few Survive." *Harvard Educational Review* 56 (1986): 1–17.
6. Dale Ballou and Michael Podgursky. *Teacher Pay and Teacher Quality* (Kalamazoo, MI: W. E. UpJohn Institute, 1997).
7. Ellen R. Delisio, "Pay for Performance: What Went Wrong in Cincinnati?" *Education World,* http://www.educationworld.com/a_issues/issues/issues374b.shtml (accessed October 24, 2006).
8. William Sanders and Sandra Horn, "Research Findings from the Tennessee Value-Added Assessment System (TVAS) Database: Implications for Educational Evaluation and Research," *Journal of Personnel Evaluation in Education* 12:3(1998): 247–56.
9. Thomas Kane and Douglas Staiger, "The Promises and Pitfalls of Using Imprecise School Accountability Measures," *Journal of Economic Perspectives* 16:4 (2002): 91–114.
10. Dee and Keys 2004 "Does Merit Pay Reward Good Teachers?"
11. David Figlio and Lawrence Kenny, "Individual Teacher Incentives and Student Performance," *Journal of Public Economics* 91:5 (June 2007): 901–14.
12. Robert Reichardt, *Recruiting and Retaining Teachers with Alternative Pay*, Aurora, CO: McREL research report, 2002.

13. Michael Janofsky, "Denver Teachers: A Pay for Performance Plan" *New York Times*, September 10, 1999, A16.

Chapter 2

1. National Commission on Teaching and America's Future, *What Matters Most: Teaching for America's Future* (New York: National Commission on Teaching and America's Future, 1996).
2. Stephen E. Ambrose, *Citizen Soldiers: The U.S. Army from the Normandy Beaches to the Bulge to the Surrender of Germany* (New York: Simon and Schuster, 1997), 441.
3. Personal communication with Don Kortz, July 26, 2006. All following Kortz quotations are taken from this communication.
4. Personal communication with Stephen Shogan, August 10, 2006. All following Shogan quotations are taken from this communication.
5. TURN, "About TURN, TURN Exchange," www.turnexchange.net (accessed October 10, 2006).
6. Personal communication with Bruce Dickinson, September 6, 2006. All following Dickinson quotations are taken from this communication.
7. Personal communication with Irv Moskowitz, November 10, 2006.
8. NCTAF, *What Matters Most*, 95.
9. William Sanders, James Ashton, and Paul Wright, "Comparison of the Effects of NB-PTS Certified Teachers with Other Teachers on the Rate of Student Academic Progress," technical report, National Board for Professional Teaching Standards, March 2005.
10. Douglas McGray, "Working with the Enemy," *New York Times*, Education Life Supplement, January16, 2005, 28.
11. Michael Janofsky, "Denver Teachers: A Pay-for-Performance Plan, *New York Times*, September 10, 1999, A18.
12. Carlos Illescas, "Teachers OK New DPS Contract, Pay for Performance Watched Nationwide," *Denver Post*, September 11, 1999, B01.
13. Personal communication with Bill Slotnik, October 24, 2006. All following Slotnik quotations are taken from this communication.
14. See Frederick Hess, "Introduction," *Educational Entrepreneurship: Realities, Challenges, Possibilities* (Cambridge, Harvard Education Press, 2006), 14–16.
15. Personal communication with Les Woodward, August 3, 2006. All following Woodward quotations are taken from this communication.
16. Rose Community Foundation internal document, October 19, 1999.
17. Copy of letter sent to Board of Education, Rose Community Foundation internal document, January 26, 2000.
18. Brian Weber, "Foundation offers $1 Million for Teacher Pay," *Rocky Mountain News*, February 2, 2000, 4.
19. Carlos Illescas, "Denver Schools Given Grant for Teacher Pay," *Denver Post*, February 2, 2000, 4B.
20. Illescas, "Denver Schools Given Grant."

21. Personal communication with Elaine Berman, August 26, 2006.
22. Editorial, "Rescuing Performance Pay," *Rocky Mountain News*, February 5, 2000, 36.

Chapter 3

1. Personal communication with Bill Slotnik, October 25, 2006. All following Slotnik quotations are taken from this communication.
2. Personal communication with Jerry Wartgow, October 11, 2006. All following Wartgow quotations are taken from this communication.
3. Personal communication with Veronica Davey, October 11, 2006.
4. Personal communication with Jeff Buck, October 24, 2006. All following Buck quotations are from this communication.

Chapter 4

1. Community Training and Assistance Center (CTAC). *Catalyst for Change: Pay for Performance in Denver* (Denver: Community Training and Assistance Center, 2004).
2. CTAC, *Catalyst for Change*, 11.
3. CTAC, *Catalyst for Change*, 5.
4. Personal communication with Bruce Dickinson, September 6, 2006.
5. Personal communication with Jeff Buck, October 24, 2006. Following quotations from Buck are taken from this communication.
6. ProComp Agreement between DPS and DCTA, 8.
7. ProComp Agreement, 6, 7.
8. ProComp Agreement, 9.
9. ProComp Agreement.
10. CTAC, *Catalyst for Change*, 144.
11. Personal communication with Becky Wissink, September 5, 2006. Following quotations from Wissink are taken from this communication.
12. Rose Community Foundation internal document, February 12, 2006.
13. Rose Community Foundation internal document.
14. Personal communication with Lydia Peña, September 15, 2006.
15. Personal communication with Sheila Bugdanowitz, October 1, 2006.
16. Personal communication with Veronica Davey. October 11, 2006. All following quotations from Davey are taken from this communication.
17. Personal communication with Steve Welchert, September 6, 2006.
18. Personal communication with John Britz, September 6, 2006. All following quotations from Britz are taken from this communication.
19. Personal communication with Greg Ahrnsbrak, September 11, 2006. All following quotations from Ahrnsbrak are taken from this communication.
20. Personal communication with Chrisanne LaHue, September 11, 2006. Following quotations from LaHue are taken from this communication.
21. Personal communication with Beth Douma, September 11, 2006.

22. Personal communication with Beverly Ausfahl, October 26, 2006.
23. Nancy Miller, "Pay Plan Gets a Gold Star," *Rocky Mountain News*, March 20, 2004, A3.
24. Miller, "Pay Plan Gets a Gold Star."

Chapter 5

1. Personal communication with Becky Wissink, September 5, 2006. All following Wissink quotations are from this communication.
2. Personal communication with Bruce Dickinson, October 3, 2006. All following Dickinson quotations are from this communication.
3. Personal communication with Greg Ahrnsbrak, November 10, 2006.
4. Personal communication with Beverly Ausfahl, October 26, 2006. All following Ausfahl quotations are from this communication.
5. Personal communication with Bill Slotnik, October 25, 2006.
6. Personal communication with John Britz, September 6, 2006.
7. Personal communication with Lydia Peña, September 15, 2006.
8. Allison Sherry, "Union President a Lightning Rod for DPS Teachers," *Denver Post*, June 28, 2004, B1, B3.
9. Ibid.
10. Personal communication with Jerry Wartgow, October 25, 2006
11. See Allison Sherry, "DPS, Teachers Announce Details of Tentative Labor Deal, *Denver Post*, April 22, 2005, B3.
12. Editorial, "DPS, Teachers Strike Welcome Agreement," *Denver Post*, April 22, 2005, B6; Editorial, "Whew: DPS Avoids Strike with Contract," *Rocky Mountain News*, April 22, 2005, 46A.
13. Personal communication with Bruce Benson, October 3, 2006.
14. Personal communication with Sheila Bugdanowitz, October 30, 2006.
15. Annette Espinoza, "Sen. Salazar Gets behind DPS Teacher Pay Proposal." *Denver Post*, October 2, 2005, C3.
16. Personal communication with Greg Kolomitz, October 29, 2006.

Chapter 6

1. Personal communication with Jeff Buck, October 24, 2006.
2. Personal communication with Andre Pettigrew, October 16, 2006. All following Pettigrew quotations are from this communication.
3. *The Denver Plan,* Denver Public Schools, February 1, 2006, 4 (available at http://thedenverplan.dpsk12.org).
4. Personal communication with Connie White, October 18, 2006.
5. Personal communication with Ed Freeman, October 16, 2006.
6. Personal communication with Josh Allen, October 16, 2006.
7. Steven D. Levitt and Stephen J. Dubner. *Freakonimics: A Rogue Economist Explores the Hidden Side of Everything* (New York: William Morrow, 2005), 19–51.

8. Levitt presentation to Public Education and Business Coalition annual luncheon at the Hyatt Regency, Denver, May 3, 2006.
9. Personal communication with Kim Ursetta, October 30, 2006. All following Ursetta quotations are from this communication.

Chapter 7

1. Personal communication with Bill Slotnik, October 25, 2006. Following Slotnik quotation comes from this conversation.
2. Frederick Hess, ed., *With the Best of Intentions: How Philanthropy is Reshaping K-12 Education* (Cambridge, MA: Harvard Education Press, 2005).
3. Personal communication with Bruce Dickinson, November 3, 2006.

Chapter 8

1. See, for example, Frederick Hess, *Spinning Wheels: The Politics of Urban School Reform* (Washington, DC: Brookings Institution Press, 1999).
2. Paul Sabatier and Hank Jenkins-Smith, eds., *Policy Change and Learning: An Advocacy Coalition Approach* (Boulder, CO: Westview Press, 1993). On incrementalism, see also Charles Lindblom, "The Science of Muddling Through," *Public Administration Review* 19 (1959): 78–88.
3. Frank Baumgartner and Bryan Jones, *Agenda and Instability in American Politics* (Chicago: University of Chicago Press, 1993).
4. John Kingdon, *Agendas, Alternatives, and Public Policies* (New York: HarperCollins, 1995).
5. Mark Schneider and Paul Teske, *Public Entrepreneurs: Agents for Change in American Government* (Princeton, NJ: Princeton University Press, 1995).
6. Joseph Schumpeter, *Capitalism, Socialism, and Democracy* (New York: Harper, 1942), 82–85.
7. Psychological work on the need for control that entrepreneurs seem to have includes: James Rotter, "Generalized Expectations for Internal versus External Control of Reinforcement," *Psychological Monographs* 80 (1966): 609–23; and Robert Brockhaus and Pamela Horwitz, "The Psychology of the Entrepreneur" in *The Art and Science of Entrepreneurship*, ed. Donald L. Sexton and Raymond W. Smilor (Cambridge: Ballinger, 1986), 25–48. Building on this work, James Welsh and John White listed 11 common characteristics of entrepreneurs in their essay "Converging of Characteristics of Entrepreneurs" in *Frontiers of Entrepreneurship Research*, ed. Kenneth Vesper (Wellesley, MA: Babson College, 1981), 29–58.
8. Data from a 1995 Panel Study of Entrepreneurial Dynamics, focused upon business entrepreneurs compared to a control group, suggests that entrepreneurs are not extreme risk takers but are less likely to perceive a downside to their opportunities than others and more often frame risks as potential gains.
9. Robert Brown and Jeffrey R. Cornwall, *The Entrepreneurial Educator* (Lanham, MD: Scarecrow Press: 2000), 11.

10. Sara Mead and Renee Rybak, "Innovator of the Year: *21st Century Schools Project Bulletin* 4, no. 24 (December 21, 2004) http://www.ppionline.org/ppi_ci.cfm?knlgAreaI D = 110&subsecID = 900001&contentID = 253092 (accessed October 20, 2006).
11. For a summary of recent philanthropic efforts in education across the nation, see Frederick Hess, ed., *With the Best of Intentions: How Philanthropy Is Reshaping K–12 Education* (Cambridge, MA: Harvard Education Press, 2005).
12. William Riker, *The Art of Political Manipulation* (New Haven, CT: Yale University Press, 1986).
13. Joe Williams, "Entrepreneurs within School Districts," in Hess, *Educational Entrepreneurship*, 125–44.

Glossary of Key Terms and Acronyms

AFT—American Federation of Teachers
CEA—Colorado Education Association
CSAP—Colorado Student Assessment Program
CTAC—Community Training and Assistance Center
DCTA—Denver Classroom Teachers Association
DPS—Denver Public Schools
JTF—Denver's Joint Task Force on Teacher Compensation
NEA—National Education Association
NCLB—No Child Left Behind—2001 federal legislation
NCTAF—National Commission on Teaching and America's Future
PDU—professional development units
PFP—pay for performance plans
Rose—Rose Community Foundation
TAP—Teacher Assistance Plan, Milken Foundation
TIF—Teacher Incentive Fund, U.S. Department of Education
TURN—Teachers Union Reform Network

ProComp Cast of Characters

Greg Ahrnsbrak—DPS teacher organizer

Rich Allen—DPS associate superintendent, 2001–06

Beverly Ausfahl—ProComp organizer and former CEA president

Michael Bennet—DPS superintendent, 2005–present

Bruce Benson—DPS Foundation chair, businessman, and former chair of
    Colorado's Republican Party

Elaine Berman—DPS board president, 1999–2003

John Britz—ProComp campaign consultant

Jeff Buck—DPS teacher, DCTA leader, ProComp JTF member

Sheila Bugdanowitz—Rose Community Foundation president and CEO,
    1999–present

Veronica Davey—Broad Foundation program officer

Bruce Dickinson—DCTA executive director, 1988–present

Beth Douma—DPS teacher organizer

Cal Frazier—ProComp liaison and former Colorado commissioner of
    education

Ed Freeman—DPS director of technology services

Andrea Giunta—DCTA president, 1998–2001

Phil Gonring—Rose Community Foundation program officer, 1996–present

John Hickenlooper—Denver mayor, 2003–present

Eric Hirsch—former executive director of the Alliance for Quality Teaching,

Brad Jupp—DPS teacher and DCTA negotiator

Greg Kolomitz—Political consultant for ProComp citizen vote

Don Kortz—Rose Community Foundation president and CEO, 1995–98

Laura Lefkowitz—Denver Board of Education member, 1995–99

Peter Martinez—former MacArthur Foundation program officer

Irv Moskowitz—DPS superintendent, 1994–1999

Bill Owens—Colorado governor, 1998–2006

Lydia Peña—Rose Community Foundation chair of education committee

Andre Pettigrew—DPS assistant superintendent, 2001–05; COO, 2005–present

Pat Sandos—DPS administrator and ProComp design team member

Shirley Scott—ProComp design team and transition team member
Bernadette Seick—DPS interim superintendent, 2000–2001
Stephen Shogan—Rose Community Foundation founding trustee
Bill Slotnik—CTAC president, key evaluator of ProComp pilot
Paul Talmey—ProComp pollster
Paul Teske—University of Colorado professor, 2003–present
Kim Ursetta—DCTA president, 2005–present
Jerry Wartgow—DPS superintendent, 2001–05
Steve Welchert—ProComp campaign consultant
Connie White—ProComp transition team cochair
Ed Wiley—ProComp evaluation study principal investigator, 2005–present
Becky Wissink—DCTA president, 2001–05
Les Woodward—Denver Board of Education president, 2003–05
Sidney "Chip" Zullinger—DPS superintendent, 1999–2000

About the Authors

Phil Gonring is senior program officer at Rose Community Foundation in Denver. He was integrally involved in the development of ProComp and continues to lead the philanthropic community's efforts to implement it. He is a former teacher, a founding lead teacher (coprincipal) of the Rocky Mountain School of Expeditionary Learning (one of the first New American Schools), and the author of book chapters on experiential education, teacher appraisal, and a magazine article on school choice. Gonring was formerly the cochair and president of the board of directors for Grantmakers for Education.

Paul Teske is professor of public affairs and director of the Center for Education Policy Analysis at the School of Public Affairs at the University of Colorado at Denver and Health Sciences Center. He won the 2005 Distinguished Research Award from the National Association of Schools of Public Affairs and Administration. Teske's coauthored book on education, *Choosing Schools* (Princeton University Press, 2000, with M. Schneider and M. Marschall), won the Wildavsky Award for best policy book of 2000-01. He has published chapters in several books from Brookings Institution Press and a chapter in *Educational Entrepreneurship* (edited by R. Hess, Harvard Education Press, 2006). His recent research has focused on school choice, leadership, and finance.

Brad Jupp is senior academic policy advisor to Denver Public Schools (DPS) superintendent Michael Bennet. For six years Jupp served as a union representative and teacher leader in the collaborative effort between DPS and its teachers union to create ProComp. From 2000 to 2004, Jupp was team leader of the DPS/DCTA Pay for Performance Design Team, the body that helped develop ProComp. Jupp has been a DPS employee since 1987; his most recent classroom assignment was as lead teacher at the Alternative Middle School of the DPS Contemporary Learning Academy.

Index